For my parents.
Thank you for forcing me to work at the Drycleaner's.
I think it really helped build my character.

Table of Contents

Forward

Personal Finance matters to me because I absolutely sucked at it in the years after I graduated from College and first got a job. Since then, I've tried to earnestly, and intentionally educate myself about important subjects within this area, and now, would like to share this information with other people who might be in the position that I once was. I'll use this opening to also add a blanket disclaimer that all the opinions within this book are entirely my own, and that I am, by no means, a personal finance guru, nor do I hold any fancy certificates like a CFP. Still, I promise you, that nowhere in this book will you find a pitch about either selling knives out of your trunk, or getting involved in some leadership scheme that will require you to enroll 20 people from your social network within the next 24-48 hours. Instead, what you will find is a collection of the missteps I took, and the knowledge I slowly acquired over my first few years managing my own finances. Discussed are some successes, some failures, but all experiences that benefited my understanding of how money works, how to build wealth, and how to attain a greater degree of happiness as a young twenty-something making the transition from adolescence to adulthood.

To understand why I've formatted this book the way that I have, it's important to see where my perspective is coming from. There are many people who are extremely financially savvy because they either pursued a business-related degree, in which learning about financial concepts was a requirement, or had the personal drive to educate themselves on financial topics. I am not one of those people. I had absolutely none of that drive, nor did I pursue a finance degree while in school. Honestly, I knew nothing about how money worked for the first twenty or so years of my life. In my defense, during my formative years, I was preparing myself to go through years of post-graduate education, and though I realize now how naïve of an assumption this really was, I always just assumed that I wouldn't have to learn about finances until I was an "adult".

It's a bit ironic, but the primary reason I wanted to enter a professional career, and do post-graduate training, was because I believed that going down this path was a solid means of financial success. I had this unicorn vision that if I became a doctor, money would just "handle" itself, and so, I shouldn't waste precious studying time trying to learn about whatever the heck the stock market was. On a more personal level, at this point, I wasn't even questioning whether there were other career paths that were better suited for me, rather, I just thought that all career professionals had successful lives, and that this is the path that I should head down.

That belief led me to be quite studious throughout high school, and eventually into College, where I majored in Biology, hoping to enter medicine. Flash forward to four years later, I had a solid GPA, but absolutely zero passion for committing to 8-12 years of postgraduate training in a profession that I didn't feel a particular calling for. By this time, I'd done a couple hundred hours of physician shadowing and I saw that the doctors that I could relate to, the ones who'd entered the profession to attain a certain lifestyle, ended up being very worn out and dispassionate people. I eventually realized that the trade-off that they'd made had been seriously ill advised, and it was something that I did not want to do. Now, I'm not saying that pursuing post-graduate studies is the *wrong* choice, but I am saying that it was the wrong choice for *me*. For some people, having the passion to pursue these careers is more than enough to carry them through the grueling training. But, I didn't have that. I finally made the decision to not pursue postgraduate education, and subsequently entered the job market. This was when a whole cascade of finance-related research began for me.

I'm not going to lie, I was sort of at a standstill after I graduated. I had absolutely no idea as to how to find a job. Other than receiving advice from my professors to enter a master's program in microbiology, I had absolutely zero career direction. In the months of joblessness post-graduation, I felt like a failure. It was funny because up until then, I'd always considered myself to be "smart" because I was continually at the top of my class, but now, I was slowly realizing just how ridiculously dumb I'd been all those years. It was difficult to stomach the fact that because I had subjected myself to being in this insular cocoon for so many years, where my only focus in life was to study organic chemistry, I let important topics like financial planning, mental health, and overall happiness go out the window for a solid 5-6 years of my life. So, at 22, a fresh, jobless graduate, with education debt, I had a ton of thinking to do, which would ultimately be the impetus for a lot of personal growth. People who I had dismissed because they weren't serious about school were the ones who'd gone to all the career fairs and were now working in awesome companies. This was a humbling time for me because it opened my eyes to this air of superiority I'd always carried within myself, and showed me a new humility that I didn't know that I desperately needed. Throughout this time, I realized that, though quite a difficult undertaking, introspection is a worthy endeavor, and always leaves you a better person.

I started pondering questions that I thought I wouldn't have to think about for the next decade. What is a 401(k)? Should I contribute to my Roth, Traditional, or both? How do I even get a Roth, can I buy it at a gas station? What is auto-deposit, and how do I figure out my bank routing number? While all of these questions seem basic to the master of personal finance, they can come all at once and be a huge, unwelcome, burden to the unassuming College student whose current highlight in life is finding free slices of pizza around campus.

While this pondering eventually helped me, at the onset, this overwhelming burden caused me to enter a phase of my life that I would entitle as "Paralysis by Analysis." I tried to answer these questions about personal finance, and even more general questions like what type of job I should get, or the industries in which I was even employable. To the point where I bought this huge piece of stock paper, and wrote out the pros and cons of 7 different career options, immediately got overwhelmed, promptly threw it in the garage, and remained jobless for another 2 months. As you can tell, this was a weird stage in my life, because before, I'd had ALL the answers, whereas now, I felt like I didn't know anything.

This outlook on life, where everything is bleak, and it's just easier to sit in your basement, eat flaming hot Cheetos, and binge watch an entire season of a French sci-fi show, is surprisingly prevalent. Well, maybe not that specifically relevant, but you get it! If it's not a French sci-fi show, it might be something a bit more blasé. But what, can I say? There are some amongst us that are simply, thespians, and like to enjoy a wide variety of international programm...ok I'm going to stop.

Anyways, the worst part about this time in my life was that there was not one clear, concise source of information that I could rely on, so even research seemed overwhelmingly daunting. On Monday, I vaguely understood what mutual funds were, and on Tuesday, I read a contradicting article article and went back to knowing absolutely nothing about them. At a certain point, this lack of "success" at understanding what everyone else seems to be doing so effortlessly, leads to resentment, and ultimately recklessness.

Recklessness in the sense that after that resentment wanes, you start to grow complacent, "Well I'm making money, why do I need to understand how any of this stuff works? I'll focus on it when I'm 30." So now, the salary you're banking monthly turns into 100% expense, and in some cases, an even scarier situation where a person lands in serious debt because they're trying to live a lifestyle that is well beyond their means. In the age of Instagram, where personal image is everything, this is a concept that has become more prevalent now, than it was in years past.

This book is a detailed account of how I largely avoided the recklessness that comes with bad financial moves, and moved beyond the resentment and complacency into a mindset of empowered mindfulness about both the amount of money I make, how I make that money work for me, and how I live happily and comfortably within my means. It's an attempt at putting that incoherent, jumbled set of actions that led me from that initial sense of extreme anxiety over assuming this newfound responsibility to now, where I generally traverse it more responsibly. Ok, so French sci-fi binging is still a pretty prominent part of my life, but hey, cut me some slack, that stuff is good!

Chapter 1:
Student Loans & Debt

When I was in College, I worked many odd jobs to supplement my spending money and to offset my tuition costs. I worked as a Resident Advisor, as a part-time Research Assistant at the library, did tutoring work for professors and even had a brief stint at Chick-fil-a! The chicken grease and lunch rush were a bit much for me. At the time, I had a pretty small budget filled with primarily three categories: entertainment, food, and school. One thing I noticed after leaving school was that there is a distinct psychological shift when you go from having no money to suddenly having a "ton" of (more accurately, comparably more) money. This psychological shift encourages more erratic money behaviors and can become a dangerous habit if not addressed. To understand this shift, it's important to look at the differences between budgeting on a small, manageable scale where you have relatively nonexistent living costs, and the more realistic, and considerably larger, scale that most adults manage day-to-day.

And so, I want to talk more about the specifics of the mad money I was raking in while at College, and compare the habits that I had then with the habits I developed once I got a full-time job and became a salaried employee. So, from my RA job, I got paid $35 every week, and no, I did not graduate in 1948. Though it seems ludicrous, this paltry stipend SORT of made sense because we got free housing (not a meal plan though...what's that about?). From my part-time library job, I got paid roughly $2,000 a semester in work study dollars, which ended up being a roundabout figure of about $125 a week. And lastly, from my teaching assistantship, I got paid $2,500 a semester as well, which was paid in a lump sum, but ended up being around $125 a week. So, all in all, I had a working salary of $280 per week, which is actually not that bad for a College student.

Though I was a total idiot throughout most of my time in College, I did make one sound decision which was allocating roughly half of my earnings from sophomore year and junior year to offsetting my book and tuition costs. Though it wasn't my intention at the time, that money contributed towards my tuition each semester ended up helping me immensely down the road because it meant I didn't have to take out another $12,000 in loans. So please, if you're in College, and you have the choice of buying a brown recliner, that will no doubt be filled with dubious stains by the end of College, or paying your tuition and not taking out extra loans, pick the latter! Eventually, when I graduated, I had about $12,000 in loans, which was helped with a hefty scholarship during the first two years I was in school, and all the jobs I worked. Had I chosen to be reckless with my spending, I could've potentially graduated with $24,000+ in loans, making that repayment period much longer, and leeching away more of my hard-earned money via interest fees.

Speaking to budgeting, at the end of the day, after paying tuition costs, I was normally left with about $130 to work with on a week-to-week basis, and I made it work. I can't remember a time in College when I felt particularly "strapped for cash" because my mindset was already frugal. I spent about $25 on groceries per week, and was even able to make it through an entire three months in a foreign country on about $400, though my dad bailed me out right at the end and I WAS able to afford that $75 bus ticket to Bali (thanks dad). Generally speaking, I developed a mindset that allowed me to avoid the luxuries of life because I knew they were out of my budget.

If I were to sum up how different my perspective on money became in the weeks after I got a FT job, I'd say it's best explained by my lunch. Lunch? Yeah! Lunch! How much I chose to spend on my lunch is really a representation of how out of whack my spending became in the months after I graduated. When I was in school, buying a $14-16-dollar lunch seemed like such an extravagance (and it is!). If I'd done that in College, one lunch would be about 13% of my entire budget for that week! But suddenly, you go from having little to no money to having a ton of disposable cash once you get your first job. My first job out of College was teaching in public schools, so admittedly, my salary was not very high at all. But there's something about seeing a direct deposit of $2,000 hit your bank account that sort of rattles your brain. I'd never seen that much money, at one time, in my bank account, ever! I would be lying if I said I didn't spend $10-25 on FOOD every day for absolutely too long. The first few paychecks I got, I blew entirely on meaningless stuff.

I'm not exactly sure why it was so second nature for me to automatically switch from that relatively frugal mindset in College, where I was buying $1 Doritos locos tacos to spending $16 on a casual lunch on a Wednesday after work, when I could've easily gone home and cooked something myself. Suddenly, I had a car payment, gas costs, insurance, both medical and auto, and I stopped bumming off my roommate's aunt's ex-boyfriend's mom's Netflix, and got my own subscription. These new expenses, coupled with bad spending habits that

I'd developed rather quickly, created a mess of a situation. My wakeup call was when I calculated my expenses during my third or fourth month on the job, after growing frustrated that I'd only been able to save $500 over that entire span of time, and realized that I still had a ton of student loans to pay off. After tallying it up, I saw that I was regularly spending 80-90% of my salary each month, and that too, while living with my parents. I was shocked, and felt like an idiot, but I took a lesson from it.

This realization caused me to reevaluate my priorities. Sitting at my desk, looking at all the table plants I'd bought, I was disgusted with myself. I still had thousands of dollars of student debt to dig myself out of, and I was being a complete child and buying anything that I wanted. This situation is one that many of us fall into – regardless of whether or not we go to College. The reason I added the "Debt" portion to the end of this chapter's name is because I understand that not everyone chooses to go to College, but, I'm also aware of the fact that most people end up in debt. While 70% of College graduates leave school with school loans looming over their head, a very comparable 80% of the general population is in debt, so this is a problem that most of society faces. Making matters worse, with the increased ease of taking out credit these days, younger people are accumulating massive amounts of debt, and this is a horrible reality to build in one's life, especially that early on.

My opinion is that you should try to dig yourself out of debt as soon as possible, and that debt is something that you try to consciously avoid throughout your life (excluding normal financial decisions like a mortgage or a car payment, which should not be equated to credit card debt or student loans). Even though I was relatively slow moving on having that realization, once I finally did understand that message, I buckled down. As I stated earlier, I graduated with $12,000 in student loans, which might seem like a lot to some, and a very small amount to others. The average credit card balance of most people sits at around $6,375, so there's a reference point for you. All in all, I was able to pay off my entire $12,000 in student loans within 1 year of graduating. Yes, I lived with my parents. Yes, there was a 9-month period where I devoted 90% of my paycheck to my student loans. Yes, the "fun" activity in my life at the time was a once-a-month treat at the movies. And yes, even more frustratingly, most of my "free" cash was being spent on the gas and car lease that I needed to get from my house to my job. Many of my friends at the time thought that I was being extreme because we had years to pay off this loan. For me, it was a calculated financial decision. Today, years later, those same friends are paying minimums on a $10,000 student loan they could've said goodbye to and paid off in full had they not bought the 30th succulent off Amazon. You have to prioritize!

Now, based on the type of student loan you receive, you'll have a set "grace" period, in which you're given the time to get financially settled before starting repayment. One of the best parts of this grace period is that for most loans, there is absolutely no interest accrual during this time. All the loans that I took out were federal loans, direct subsidized, so they already had low interest rates, but as an added bonus, they also came with good grace periods. Based on the amount you take out, you might have to go for private loans, which are a completely different ballgame, so doing the appropriate research is of utmost importance if you want to be as cost efficient as possible.

To give an accurate example, most federal loans give you anywhere between 10 to 25 years to pay off the entirety of the loan. For an extreme example, let's say I chose to pay off my $12,000 loan over 25 years. I'd end up paying, over the lifetime of that loan, $20,400, which means I'd have basically paid over 50% of my original loan in interest! The larger the loan amount, the crazier that number gets. So yes, while that first year was painful, and I didn't get to go to Austin City Limits, I also don't have any student loans today, and I honestly much rather prefer the latter. This same dedication to frugality can be applied to personal credit card loans. Overall, one of the best decisions I made was taking advantage of that grace period, paying all my loans off within that time frame, and never paying a dime in interest.

Another point of discussion is setting up multiple streams of income. In addition to salaried work, you can increase your monthly earnings by exploring different income streams, something that is discussed in subsequent chapters within this book. Also, start considering ways to lower your living expenses so that you're able to devote more money to paying off that debt. Examples of this include living with roommates, or possibly even at home in the year after graduating from school, if that's a possibility.

One last thing to note is that aggressively tackling loan payments is something that works for people who have more manageable loan amounts. One aspect of student loans that not many students consider is loan forgiveness programs. During my time as a teacher, I met colleagues who had loans in excess of $100,000, and had entered the teaching profession so that they could receive benefits of loan forgiveness programs. All in all, figuring out a system to free yourself of debt, whether that be through repayment or through entering a repayment program, will significantly increase your overall quality of life.

<u>Key Takeaways</u>

✓ When you're in College, do your best to choose a school you're happy with, but as importantly, chose one that won't leave you debilitated with debt **afterwards**!

✓ Try to maximize any scholarships + work studies, so that you're able to offset your end-of-school tuition bill.

✓ If you graduate with a manageable amount of debt (x<$50,000), devote your first 1-3 years post-grad to paying that off in **FULL**. Take advantage of the grace period, don't make minimums, and say sayonara to something that could turn into a lifetime payment if not addressed **immediately.**

✓ Don't be fooled by "mad money" you start raking in post-grad. You're still likely making $50,000 per year, most of which needs to go to your debt payments. Stop buying succulents! <u>Say no to the brunch, $40 IS a big deal</u>!

✓ Until you've methodically started tackling your debt, and have made a large enough dent, it's not yet time to allocate your money to investment, focus on paying off your debt **FIRST**.

Chapter 2:
Make your Credit Cards work for you

I was at a party the other night, when one of my close friends from College said to me, "I don't use credit cards because I don't feel responsible enough and just don't want to complicate my life." I was shocked. This friend of mine, in all respects, is massively more "adult" than I have ever been. While I was more of the, "waking up at 8 AM for an 8:15 AM midterm" type of person, this friend was meticulous, grounded, and earnest, three ideals that most College students rarely embody. Soon after we graduated, I stumbled into my momentary lapse of judgement and began spending erratically and staying up until 2AM when I had a 7AM classroom full of middle schoolers to teach (old habits die hard), whereas my friend got married, moved into an apartment, and started graduate school. So, when I heard him, who was arguably the most mature friend I had, say that he'd had never had a credit card, I realized the true pervasiveness of misconceptions regarding credit cards within society.

Yes, to his credit, I will admit that credit cards can land people in a ton of debt. If you take out credit at an early age, without any related education, you're putting yourself in a very precarious situation. To give you an example, for every friend I had in College that was very mature like the friend described above, I probably had five more that were falling into credit card hell. Most of the issue is related to access to a large amount of money, seemingly out of thin air, but in and of itself, the belief that you "own" this money is a delusion. Basically, when you sign up for a card, you get pre-approved up to a certain ceiling. For most people starting out, that limit is around $2,500. Now, that doesn't mean that this entitles you to $2,500! I had friends who bought new $30,000 cars while sophomores in College, without a job! They financed it entirely through, you guessed it, credit cards! The correct approach to credit cards is to treat them no differently than a debit card, spend what you have at all times.

While my friend has reason to be apprehensive, it's imperative that someone who is looking to own a house, financed through a mortgage, and live within mainstream society has a credit card by the age of 18, or even younger if possible. There's a couple of different reasons for this, the primary one being your credit score. A credit score is a metric that is comprised of a bunch of varying factors, an example of which is the oldest age of one of your credit lines, the older the relationship, the bigger the boost to your credit score. On top of that, you build credit by making timely payments, diversifying the type of credit you take out, and by increasing your credit limit by taking out multiple cards, though that latter part really should be avoided until you have a couple of years of responsible credit habits built up.

Now, when making the initial plunge, there are certain aspects of taking out a credit card that you should be well aware of and talk to your relationship banker about, prior to signing on any dotted lines:

Factor #1: Are you old enough? First, there's age minimums. Technically, you need to be 18 to get a credit card. However, if you have an interest in starting to build credit before that age, and it's highly recommended, become an authorized user on an adult's card. Following this path, teenagers can get approved for credit cards with the help of their parent or guardian. One important discussion that should take place between the child and guardian is the risk associated with such an agreement. First, guardians are on the hook for any irresponsible behavior their minor does, because it's their credit score that's getting dinged at the end of the day. Secondly, these joint accounts will allow for viewing access of all purchases, which can cause issues when the child feels that their privacy is being infringed upon, so a discussion of trust is imperative.

Factor #2: Should you go for a rewards card? Another factor to entice people to have credit cards, which is honestly akin to free money, is purchasing rewards. Based on the type of rewards you want (options include reward miles, gift cards, cash back, etc.), you should choose a card that provides that service and rewards you for every purchase you make with their card. One of the biggest mistakes I made was not using a rewards card for the first account that I opened. To build credit, funneling all your smaller day to day expenses through your credit card is a genius move, and it also helps to amass a huge number of rewards. Instead of using your debit card daily, which is dangerous, because your debit card getting stolen is massively worse than your credit card getting stolen, swipe using your credit card. At the end of the week, pay off the remaining credit card balance with your debit card funds, and by doing this repeatedly over weeks, months, and years, you build a great track history of on-time repayments. My idiotic move was following this approach for nearly 4 years without using a rewards card, and thereby foregoing at least a 1-2K of airline savings.

Factor #3: What is APR and how does it affect me? Moving towards speaking about the card in particular, the biggest factor to consider is the Annual Percentage Rate (APR) of the card. Usually, on loans and cards, you're given an interest rate. With credit cards, that interest rate is presented a bit differently, in that it's viewed on an annual basis, and is marketed as the APR. There's a few reasons why APR matters a ton, and why APR doesn't matter much. First, there's the fact that if you pay off your credit card balance in full on a monthly basis, APR will never affect you, because it cannot be applied to payments paid on time. However, if you have a late payment, and let that sit around for a while, APR can end up affecting you in a very serious way.

For example, an average APR hovers between 13-23%, with newer borrowers getting higher levels of APR because they don't have an established credit score. If, at the beginning of your borrowing, you rack up $5,000 in credit card debt with a 20% APR and plan to pay it off within a year, you'll end up paying about $550 in interest throughout that period. Not making timely payments, over borrowing, and then having to shell out interest payments is a sure-fire way to lose hard earned money. If you're considering a particular card, it'd be wise to use an online APR calculator to see the types of situations you could get yourself into, and if you could stomach the worst-case scenarios.

Factor #4: How do I calculate minimum repayments? Another important factor when getting a credit card, which can often be very misleading, is your minimum credit card payment. The more popular trend amongst credit card companies lately has been to offer extremely low minimum payments such as $25. When users see this on an online dashboard, they're deluded into thinking that this is the entire balance that is due at that point, and that interest will not be applied to the remaining balance. Wrong! While you can get away with paying the $25 at that time, rest assured that the interest will certainly be applied to your remaining balance. As the amount you owe gets higher and higher, your credit card company could shift this minimum payment allocation and start charging you a percentage of your total balance as a minimum. Again, as stated prior, best practice is to pay off the entirety of your bill on a weekly to bi-weekly basis, and not get used to the false sense of reassurance that paying a minimum payment provides you.

Factor #5: Do all cards charge annual fees? No! Annual fees are usually operational costs that are associated with the credit card. These fees are annual charges applied at one-time throughout a calendar year, and can range from $20-$500, depending upon how flashy or benefits-ridden your card happens to be. There are certainly cases in which you can outright avoid paying annual fees, such as cards offered through campus banking branches. However, a cost-benefit analysis must be performed to pinpoint whether getting a card with an annual fee, but a higher degree of benefits, is better for you than getting a card with no annual fee. During my search for a rewards card, I found a card that provided me with roughly $400 in annual miles per year, but had an annual fee of $100. Obviously, this situation was more beneficial to me than getting a card with no annual fee, as the former scenario provides me with a rough net of $300 annually. So, while it might seem like a "no-brainer" to go for a card with no annual fee, it's usually more complicated than that.

Unrelated Factor #6: Wait, what about Debit Cards? Aside from annual fees, banks can often apply charges based on certain activities performed by the account. I'm going to outline two of the biggest hitters in this category, but please be aware that the charges can be varied, so exploring this topic with your relationship banker prior to signing anything is important! It's also important to note that these two situations affect debit cards only, but they are still important to discuss because they're easy ways to lose money based on bad financial habits.

Up to bat first are overdraft charges! In the age of direct deposits, many of us have every single expense we incur on a regular basis linked to our accounts. So, in any given week, you might forget that you haven't paid your Netflix subscription yet, and accidentally buy a hoodie you know you wouldn't be able to afford if there were any additional charges made to your account before payday. Before you know it, you've over drafted, which is essentially a situation in which you've overdrawn and your account is in the negative. Usually, within a couple of hours of that happening, you have time to cancel orders and transfer money to make that account green again. But, if you don't closely monitor your account, the bank could charge you an overdraft fee if you are too late in remedying the situation. These fees are usually in the $30-40 range, which is certainly a sizeable amount of money for a small mistake. Ways to avoid this are, of course, budgeting which is discussed later in this book, but also by close monitoring of your account, which can be done by setting up text alerts from your bank, so you receive a notification the second your balance dips negative. Better still, it's a good habit to build to charge things to your credit card, so you don't incur an overdraft charge, and pay the amount off with your debit card at the end of the week. Lastly, if this situation happens, call your bank right away as the first or second time this happens, banks will usually waive the fee.

The second heavy hitter in the realm of random bank charges is ATM fees! Now, it's generally a rule of thumb that if you use an ATM of an opposing bank, domestic or international, this is considered an "out-of-network withdrawal" and you'll get charged anywhere from $3-5 per transaction, on top of the amount you're withdrawing. These fees have gotten a bit more complicated over the years, to the point now where you are charged an amount from that banking institution, but are also charged a nominal amount by the owner of that ATM, so it can push that price higher than you'd think it'd be. If you make a habit of using ATMs, it can be a huge expenditure annually, costing $200-300+ a year. Ways to avoid ATM charges are of course to know which ATMs are in network and out of network, and possibly the smartest idea is to get cash back at a point of purchase. If you're at a store, and you need cash, ask them for cash back instead of going to an ATM, because that cash back has no associated fees with it! Booyeah!

Now that you're more acquainted with the world of credit cards, it'd be smart if you started shopping around for the credit card that benefits you most. Powerful resources during this search will be online resources that compare card benefits, talking to relationship bankers at banking institutions that family members have been going to for a while, and of course exploring the specific interest rates, annual costs, and other important details associated with each card.

<u>Key Takeaways</u>

✓ As soon as you can, sign up for a credit card, and start making <u>100% on-time payment</u>s so that you can start building a **solid credit history.**

✓ Shop around! It's advantageous to look at all the different cards on the market. Weigh annual fees with *potential rewards* to see which one will give you the biggest bang for your buck.

✓ Be aware of the slimy hole that is known as the "minimum payment". Remind yourself that you need to treat your credit card like a debit card, <u>only spend what you **HAVE**</u>. Don't get into this cycle of paying dubious minimums that end up with you ponying up thousands of dollars in interest.

✓ Know how to navigate the world of debit cards! Set up banking alerts so an overdraft fee never gets you, and figure out *FREE* ways to get cash-back as opposed to paying bogus ATM fees.

Chapter 3:
First Jobs + 401(k)'s

When I got my first job as an 8th grade chemistry teacher, I was pretty fascinated with the concept that someone would PAY me a sizeable amount of money to teach kids. It was always a wild experience for me to see that money hit my account. First off, full disclaimer, I was a teacher, and that too a teacher that had just started out, so my salary was arguably one of the lowest amongst my entire peer group. Let's take a moment of silence for all the hardworking teachers out there. Though this is totally unrelated, I left teaching with an intense passion for teaching, to the point where I think anyone, anywhere, would benefit from a year spent in a teaching service. Not until I became a teacher did I realize how much life all the influential educators in my life had poured into me. So, here's a toast to all the teachers out there, as well as to the teaching colleagues that I worked with! You all are severely underappreciated, but are the beacons of our society and are doing such amazing things.

Now, swerving this vehicle back on-track, there was definitely one or two people amongst my group that rubbed in the fact that they were making a whopping 3x my salary doing banking work in New York. Note to the wise, don't care about those people, because they're more than likely 100% more insecure than you, so give them a pass and don't register their opinions at all. If you're happy doing you, that is all that matters.

In my case, I was largely unbothered because I considered having this first job a complete blessing as it provided me with more money than I'd seen in my entire life. Also, after kind of a rough start post-graduation in finding a job, I felt extremely lucky to even be employed. Now, there are certainly many intricacies related to pay, in that what you actually make on paper is much different from what you end up receiving because taxes are #REAL. Remember all those years when you heard people whining about taxes on TV? There's a reason for that. However, for the purposes of this chapter, we will focus exclusively on retirement saving.

One common experience that most newly employed people will have is the option to enter into an employer sponsored retirement plan, called a 401(k). Prior to explaining how you can maximize your own 401(k), it's useful to know a bit about the history behind this plan, and pros and cons of its radical acceptance amongst most companies and institutions in the United States. In 1978, 401(k)'s were brought in as a part of the Revenue Act of 1978. Soon after, in the early 80's, slow adoption of the plan started out, to the point where today, 90%+ of all U.S. companies and institutions offer them. There's definitely a lot of back and forth debate on how 401(k)'s are actually bad substitutions for what was a much stronger retirement option in earlier years, known as pensions. Pension systems are still very popular in Europe, but within the United States, you'll find them at less than 5% of employers, most of which are tied to federal institutions. Pensions are often touted as being more practical for the individual, as they are more amenable to budgeting, and they don't require lifetime projections like 401(k)'s do, which are generally very difficult to predict. That having been said, even in the heyday of pensions, less than 50% of people had access to this type of retirement savings. So, whereas pensions were beneficial for the few, in years past, 401(k)'s make retirement savings accessible to the many, today.

Understanding the 401(k) Match. Getting into what a 401(k) is, it's a system in which an employee can set aside pre-tax money into an investing plan, which is sponsored by the employer. Most companies choose to offer their employees investing services from large companies that specialize in 401(k) management, such as Vanguard. One of the biggest benefits of having a 401(k) is being able to invest pre-tax dollars. From there, employers offer a match which varies widely from employer to employer. To give you an idea of the wide variety of match options, some companies might limit it to a dollar amount, whereas others will match up to a certain percentage of your contributed amount (e.g. 50% up to 6% of your entire contributed limit). Having the human resources division at your work explain the contribution terms to you in plain English is imperative, because you will have to have a sound understanding of the terms at play if you plan on maximizing your match, which is "free money" offered by your employer. To give you an example, if you start out with a salary of $40,000, and your employer matches 50% of your contribution up to 8% of your salary, they will essentially be matching 4% of your total income. To maximize your 401(k) match, it would then be imperative for you to put in at least $3,200, or 8% of your income, so that you receive a matching contribution of $1,600 from your employer.

Annual Salary: $40,000
Employer Match: 50% up to 8% of your salary
Maximizing your match: $40,000 x (.08) = $3,200
Employer Match: (.50) x $3,200 = $1,600
Total Annual contribution: $3,200 + $1,600 = $4,800

Being Aware of 401(k) Contribution Limits. Each year, the Internal Revenue Service (IRS) puts out new limits for 401(k) contributions. While these limits don't change that often, and even when they do, not by much, it's important that you know them, because over contributing can cause you to incur penalties. As of 2018, the annual contribution limit sits at $18,500. This seems like a ton of money for someone starting out, who likely has a salary that is less than $50,000, but over time, as one starts to make a higher salary, it's likely that they'll start contributing on or around that number.

In relation to contribution, if you're still living with your parents, and have paid off most of your loans, try to hit that contribution limit. As discussed in later chapters, the benefits of investing early are massive, so the larger the amount, the bigger the benefit. Second, one of the great things about an employer offered 401(k) program is that you can allocate the percentage of your **pre-tax** income that you'd like to allocate to your 401(k), so it gets automatically excised before your paycheck even hits your account. That way, it really does become easier to live with a smaller paycheck, because you get used to the smaller amount over time, and budget accordingly.

Now, though this problem of over contributing to your 401(k) isn't one that many people face, there are a couple of ways to get out of it if you do find yourself in this situation. First, after you file your taxes, and realize that you over contributed, you have six months to take that excess out, and file an amended return. However, a much more preferable alternative is to just contribute less the following year. For example, if you accidentally contributed $19,000 in Year 1, just contribute $18,000 the following year so that the average contributed over the two years still falls on the current contribution limit of $18,500. There are a few caveats to this depending upon how much you went over, and you might have to pay a penalty tax until your contributions evenly average out. Discussing these issues with a Certified Public Accountant (CPA), should you run into this problem, would be a good bet.

Switching Jobs + Penalties of Cashing Out too early. Unlike most people within their parent's generation, millennials have the issue of job switching to contend with. It's often portrayed in the media that the youth of today are disloyal employees who switch jobs at a rapid rate. Of course, I have personal feelings about this. First and foremost, your life and personal identity should not reside with the name of your employer. Loyalty is a concept that should be reserved for your loved ones, for people who will unfailingly be a part of your life, and care about your interests, throughout your life. So, whereas building a long-term career at a large employer is a wonderful option, society should not villainize a person for changing jobs to find work that they prefer for whatever reason. However, because job switches have become so common, it's important to know one golden rule about 401(k)'s: NEVER CASH OUT.

When switching jobs, you're given two options: cashing out, or rolling over your 401(k) savings. One important fact to know is that you cannot withdraw from your 401(k) until you're 59 and a half, and if you do, you will incur sizeable penalties. Bummer, I know. BUT, the whole point of this program really is to, in a way, force you to save for your retirement and not take any money out for a long period of time, thereby allowing for sizeable growth. Anyways, if you withdraw early, for any reason, there are massive penalties involved. First, there is a blanket 10% withdrawal fee, on top of which is the federal income tax (which depends on your income bracket), and then your state income tax rate, which of course depends on the state that you live in. For a blanket example, see below how much money you'd lose by withdrawing early on a $25,000 investment.

> **401(k) Savings:** $25,000
> **Early Withdrawal Penalty:** (.10) x $25,000 = $2,500
> **Federal Income Tax:** (.20) x $25,000 = $5,000
> **State Income Tax:** (.10) x $25,000 = $2,500
> **Take home:** $25,000 - $10,000 = $15,000

In essence, you're looking to lose somewhere in the ballpark of 40-50% of your entire 401(k) by cashing out early. This figure, however, doesn't even take into consideration the potential earnings that you're giving up. Let's say you had the above $25,000 invested by age 30. In a traditional model, with 7% annual rate of return, and no other contributions made to your 401(k) from the age of 30 forward, you're looking at around $260,000 by the time you retire at age 65. That is a whopping $235,000 that you are forgoing by pulling your investment out early and cashing out. So, it can be seen pretty easily that keeping your money invested is of utmost importance, because patience is the name of the game with investment, in general.

The far preferable alternative to cashing out is to roll over your 401(k). The best bet is rolling your current 401(k) into your new employer's 401(k), if they have one. This option is the most seamless, and provides the least burden on your wallet and potential earnings. There are usually services that your 401(k) manager provides to help you with this transition.

Now, there is a secondary option to roll your 401(k) into a Roth IRA. This is also a good bet IF your new employer doesn't provide a 401(k) plan. Please note that if you do follow this option, you will have to pay taxes on your 401(k) amount that is being rolled over, as Roth contributions are not pre-tax, whereas 401(k) contributions are.

Finally, there is the weird option of just keeping your 401(k), there. You can certainly leave your money in your old employer's 401(k) plan. Of course, you will not be able to make new contributions, and will not benefit from a match from your old employer. This course of action can become a bit messy, depending on the amount of job changes you have over the years, which is hard to predict, because you might have multiple 401(k)'s lying around. It would make the most sense to consolidate, and keep track of them in one place, though there are some people that opt to avoid the burden of rollovers and cashing out. Another big issue with plans of action like this is forgetting where one of your 401(k) accounts are stored, which is actually a pretty common mistake. This can end up being catastrophic as far as retirement savings are concerned.

Financial Advisor Services. One common add-on that many employers provide as a part of their 401(k) plan is financial planning services. Normally, most people would be put off by the service charges that these companies charge, however, if your employer offers a meeting with a financial planner for free, it's imperative that you not procrastinate, and take them up on it! Online calculators are great at helping you understand the grand scheme and general numbers associated with certain risks and investments. However, meeting with a financial advisor one-on-one will help you understand how to project out 10, 20, 30 years, and see what you need to be doing today to reach your goals by retirement. An added benefit of meeting with a Certified Financial Planner (CFP) is discussing early retirements. Most calculators project a hard age of 65 to retire, but if you're looking to retire early, it'd be helpful to get a person in there to review your numbers, and build a realistic plan for you to retire earlier that the normal projection. In all honestly, I would recommend looking for a deal on Groupon or Yelp and utilizing a CFP service even if it isn't offered by your employer, because they can often help you see gaps in your money habits, as well as educate you on mistakes you might unknowingly be making.

Wait, what if my employer doesn't offer a 401(k)? Common issue, don't worry about it! You're not at the worst job on the planet, and your peers will not move years ahead of you, but it will be a bit more difficult for you to save for retirement, and as a result you must play it smart. First of all, there's a variety of reasons why you could potentially not benefit from a 401(k). You might be a part-time employee, in which case you wouldn't qualify for your company's 401(k) plan. Secondly, you might work for a small business that is just starting out, and they're just not able to provide a plan like that yet. Whatever the reason, there are still opportunities for you to invest and start building your retirement nest, even if you don't have access to a 401(k).

First, there's the option to put your money into a Roth or Traditional IRA, a topic that is discussed extensively in a forthcoming chapter. The benefit of these accounts is that you can open them up yourselves, and though they often come with a nominal fee, the benefit far, far outweighs the cost of these rather small management costs. The downside of accounts like this is first, no employer match, which is a bummer, and secondly, there is a maximum contribution of $5,500 compared to the much larger $18,500 afforded by a 401(k) plan.

Secondly, you might have the option to benefit from either a solo 401(k) plan, or a SEP IRA, if your employer has those programs set up. These differ by type, are not overly utilized, but offer higher contribution limits. It's an option to explore if you're a business owner or an employee in a small rig where your employer offers you this option.

Lastly, there is the sound recommendation that, if possible, you should try your best to get employed by a 401(k)-offering employer. This, of course, is highly dependent on your idea of the type of life you'd like to lead. Many self-employed individuals do not rely on retirement plans to build their retirement wealth. Rather, they focus on smart personal investing to build a foundation for their future, a topic that will be discussed in forthcoming chapters.

Key Takeaways

✓ Get over your shopping addiction! Instead of buying a *million succulents* on amazon, reroute that money towards retirement funds, they'll save you so much <u>grief</u> down the road!

✓ Talk to your HR Department about the terms of your 401(k) + Employer Match so you know how to **max your contributions.**

✓ When switching jobs, remember to roll over your 401(k), people <u>lose millions of dollars</u> when they procrastinate on administrative items like this, and eventually forget where their retirement accounts are stored.

✓ <u>**NEVER CASH OUT!**</u> Unless you absolutely NEED to (e.g. in the case of a health emergency), do not cash you 401(k)! The potential losses run in the hundreds of thousands.

✓ If you don't have a 401(k)-plan offered by your employer, look for secondary investing methods like IRAs.

✓ Don't get *too* investment happy, there are serious penalties associating with contributing MORE than you're allowed to in your 401(k) for a given year.

Chapter 4:
IRAs - Roth vs Traditional

Early on in my career, my parents gave me a lot of grief over my spending. Yes, like many people my age, I had a small, tiny obsession with ordering things on Amazon. Ok, fine, I admit it! It was incessant, so much so that even though I was allocating $18,500 of my pretax salary to my 401(k), I was usually left with $0 at the end of each month because I decided to order succulent #8,393 because it was a mini cactus and it looked so cute on screen! Fast forward to two days later (prime members, where you at?), I'd be entirely disinterested in what I'd received. I later thought about how this spending addiction was probably some dopamine rush gateway I'd opened in response to online shopping, because I was purchasing items I didn't need, or maddeningly enough, want! Though I'm going to discuss budgeting in detail in a forthcoming chapter, right now I want to describe the impetus that led me to curbing my obsessive shopping habits, and ultimately, to an increase in my annual IRA contribution.

Roth IRA. It was perhaps the millionth discussion I'd had with my dad over my finances, and as per usual, he was telling me how disappointed he was that I was ordering crap on Amazon, and not putting money in my Roth IRA. This term, "Roth IRA", at that time and point, was a jumble of 7 letters that meant nothing to me. I felt very frustrated with my dad at the time, because I thought, "Hey, here I am, maxing out my 401(k), something that nobody my age was really even thinking about, and my dad is still giving me grief!" I had this warped self-view and kind of saw myself as the most responsible young adult in any 5-mile radius. My dad said something to me that day, however that showed me just how crazy my budgeting really was. He told me that I must spend at least $2,000 on food and amazon items per month. I looked at him cross-eyed, because $2,000 was essentially 3ish months of salary for me when I was in College. I admit, I might be a bit succulent crazy, but I'm not that crazy. Infuriated, I set out to prove him wrong! I downloaded all my statements from my bank and calculated it up. In fact, I'd spent $1,800 last month. $1,800!!! I split that amount up into essentials and non-essentials, and saw that, while living at home with my parents, I was giving away $1,200 to Amazon, and other absolute useless things, per month. This was an eye-opening experience, and I'm so grateful I had it at such an early time in respect to my career, because if I'd let these habits grow, I know, that by today, I'd be headed towards financial ruin.

And so, it was at this point that I begrudgingly took my dad's advice. I started out with budgeting, but the spillover effects of me realizing how much I was sleeping on my finances was that it finally got me to think about what an IRA was, and decide that I needed to open one. So, I began the journey of starting to look into what an IRA was, how it could benefit me, and how I could get started. First thing I looked at was the contribution limits, and found that establishing and maxing out an IRA is much more manageable than doing the same for a 401(k). Annually, you're able to contribute $5,500 to your IRA account, something I could've accomplished easily in 3-4 months, if I could just stop myself from buying so many damn table plants!

Now, there are a couple of different pros of IRAs, and some cons associated with them as well.

First and foremost, an obvious pro is that setting up an IRA allows you to diversify your retirement savings, by establishing an investment account separate from your 401(k) plan. This diversification is further accomplished by a range of new investment options than what's traditionally available by an employer-run plan, as the company you work for often dictates the type of investments you're open to. Now, possibly the greatest pro of IRAs is the tax-free growth afforded to you.

Prior to getting into a discussion about tax-free growth, it's important to delineate the different type of IRA options on the table, and how they're different from one another. Largely, there are two types of IRAs: Traditional and Roth. Other IRA types exist, but for the purposes of this discussion, we'll focus on the more popular roads to IRA investment.

Roth IRA. The Roth IRA is a preferred choice for many people looking to create an IRA for the first time. One of the most advantageous reasons to start investing with a Roth IRA is because of income limits. As of 2017, if you are a single person, you have to make roughly less than $118,000 and if married, you have to make less than $196,000 combined, in order to contribute to your Roth IRA. There are modified incomes that are allowed, to help people, phase out as their incomes increase. Because these income limits change so frequently, it's imperative for you to do your research and consult an accountant if your salary starts growing closer to that upper ceiling. Another large incentive to invest in a Roth IRA when you're just starting out is projecting increases in earnings throughout your life.

Essentially, one of the biggest differences between a traditional and Roth IRA is that with the Roth IRA, you pay taxes up front, meaning, you cannot allocate pre-tax dollars to your Roth IRA. Understanding this concept, and the amazing power behind it, can be a bit confusing. When looking at it right off the bat, people are more eager to contribute to a traditional IRA, as that allows for pre-tax allocation, but, personally, I think that this is a dumb move coming from a poor understanding of the benefits of both options.

Essentially, imagine you started contributing the annual $5,500 to your Roth IRA for the first (10) years of your career, when you're making a small to medium income ($50,000-$90,000). Now, the whole time you're contributing, you're utilizing after-tax dollars, so you're paying taxes on them up front, and then contributing. Later, during your retirement, you've risen ranks in your career, and now make an annual salary of $200,000, meaning you are in a much more unforgiving tax bracket than the one you were in when you started contributing to your Roth IRA. The amazing thing is, 30 or so years ago, you paid all of your taxes on those Roth contributions under your much lower income tax bracket, so now, though you're part of a much "tougher" bracket, you don't have to worry about it, because there is zero tax applied to your Roth earnings. Withdraw and enjoy!

Another possible benefit is the idea of withdrawals. Roth IRAs allow for withdrawal of your contribution, without any penalty. This process can get a bit hairy because you have to separate your earnings from your investments from your contributed amount. Additionally, it's probably NOT the best idea to withdraw money from a retirement account, when the purpose is to "set it and forget it" until retirement, but in dire situations, this is something that is a plus.

Traditional IRA. Now, as mentioned above, one of the biggest pros of a Traditional IRA is that it offers what the Roth does not: tax deductions. This means that, much like a 401(k), you can allocate pre-tax dollars to your Traditional IRA. Now, this could potentially be beneficial to the individual for a host of reasons. First, let's say you see yourself retiring at a tax bracket much lower than the one you have today. This might be a difficult scenario to envision for most people, but examples of it that I have seen in real life is someone that starts out with a professional career (banking, medicine, etc.), and is making a large income, but later becomes a personal business owner to follow a passion or become their own boss, which sometimes means taking a pay cut. If that is the case, you can avoid paying taxes now, when your bracket is essentially higher than it will be later, and then when it comes time to pay taxes, during retirement, you can pay a much lower rate. This is definitely not the traditional model, because most people make more money as they progress throughout their career, BUT, if you have the foresight and reason to believe that you will end up in a lower tax bracket, you should proceed with, and maintain, a Traditional.

However, that concept isn't true the other way around. If you start with a Roth IRA, that doesn't mean that you shouldn't ever look at a Traditional IRA. In fact, if you ever start making more money than is allowed for Roth IRA income limits, you should certainly open up a Traditional IRA, and start contributing because, even though you might be burned by high taxes upon retiring, the potential earnings are still great, and will end up cushioning your retirement nicely.

Now, one downside of a Traditional IRA is potential withdrawals. Unlike a Roth IRA, you can't withdraw your contributions from a Traditional IRA without penalties. Technically, because you never paid taxes on these contributions, as soon as you withdraw early, you'll be charged taxes, along with a 10% tax penalty, so contributor beware!

Juxtaposing Traditional IRAs with Roth IRAs. Now that we have a baseline understanding of both IRA options, as well as a down-the-road view of how these different plans end up costing us based on our personal life decisions, we can move onto a generalized discussion of how these plans vary outside of the scope of taxation and early withdrawal penalties.

To start off, there is the point of longevity of growth. With a Traditional IRA, you are forced to withdraw all your funds, and close your account at 70.5 years. This might be a bit of an issue for people who want to let their accounts sit and grow for longer than that. A smart investor, by that age, will usually have cultivated multiple streams of investments, and will gradually withdraw to support themselves financially in old age. And so, they might want to let their IRA sit in there for a while and grow until they need it, as, meanwhile, they live off another type of investment income. In that case, starting with withdrawals from a Traditional IRA might be a better bet as with a Roth IRA, there are no age distribution requirements, and you can keep your money in there, growing, for as long as you'd like. With the topic of old age, thinking about more morbid topics such as inheritance, you can rest assured that both Roth and Traditional IRAs can be converted into inherited IRAs where designated individuals can continue contributing, or chose to withdraw.

Should I get an IRA if I already have a 401(k)? Overall, my personal recommendation would be, yes, certainly, if you have extra cash, and are using it on bogus things like I was, start budgeting, and max out an IRA, as well as contributing as much to your 401(k) as you can. As a growing professional, I started my investment plan out with a Roth IRA, because I'm optimistically not sure if I will still be eligible for the income limits in say, 10 or 20 years. Additionally, money invested now, in your early 20s, will compound into a *beautiful* number come retirement, whereas money invested in your 40s or 50s might just be an "ok" number, nothing impressive!

Lastly, I'll add that from personal experience, I don't believe that you should have to pick one or the other. Regardless of what your plan is right now, life changes, and the one thing that is a tried and true strategy is diversifying your portfolio. So, it'd only be an advantageous thing to do to open both a Roth IRA as well as a Traditional IRA. The best laid plans change, but diversified portfolios stand the test of time! So, get to it! Use online services like eTrade to open your own IRA!

<u>Key Takeaways</u>

✓ Learn to manage your budget! Contributing to sources of retirement savings, like IRAs, are <u>momentously</u> more important than contributing to your overpriced miniature plant collection!

✓ Learn the differences between a Roth and a Traditional IRA, and assess your income projections from now until retirement to decide which plan is more beneficial for you to **start out with.**

✓ Understand the importance of establishing ***MULTIPLE*** sources of savings in respect to your retirement. Having a 401(k) is awesome! But having a Roth in addition, is even better.

✓ Be aware of the tax penalties associated with cashing out ear...No...<u>NEVER CASH OUT EARLY!</u>

Chapter 5:
Introduction to Budgeting

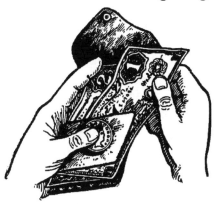

Arguably one of the biggest hallmarks of growing up and "adulting" is nailing down your budget. Like any other goal in life, this is one that should be defined and measured as much as possible. So, before we get into any of the specifics related to investment, it's really important to discuss how to enable yourself to save enough money so that you'll be able to make those investments. Of course, like any skill, you'll realize that budgeting will need to be effortfully practiced at first, but with time, will transition to being an effortless task that plays in the background CRM of your life. To start off, developing a budget in and of itself is something that's fairly simple, but sticking to that budget is where the challenge lies.

One of the biggest issues that I faced when told repeatedly, by friends and family, that I needed to develop a budget, was a complete denial of the fact that I even needed a budget. Because I was paying off my credit card bill at the end of each month, thereby incurring no month-to-month debt, I felt like I was doing really well! What I didn't realize is that friends of mine, as well as my older brothers, were saving a much greater percent of their monthly salary than I was. I've mentioned before where my wakeup call came when I calculated my monthly expenses and was ashamed by how much money I was essentially throwing into the bin every month. That wakeup call also included a month when I'd been so amazon-happy that I needed to take money out of my very meager savings account to just cover the tab I'd racked up on online shopping. If you watch "Game of Thrones", I essentially felt like Cersei being paraded through the streets..."Shame!! Shame!!" And so, I went off in pursuit of both developing a budget, as well as learning how to stick to it.

Step 1: Figure out your monthly net pay! The first aspect of budgeting involves just a very simple calculation of how much money you're bringing in on a monthly basis. For most people, with a single stream of income, this is a simple calculation. Whether you're paid biweekly, or weekly, just remember to multiple that number accordingly. The helpful part about this is you won't have to deduct any taxes mathematically, all the social security tax, and other related taxes, is taken out of your pay if you receive it via direct deposit or as a check. For others who've established multiple streams of income, as well as people that get paid by cash for services, their month-to-month pay might not always be the same, so they will have to add these numbers on a monthly basis, and excise taxes where relevant, in order to get an accurate representation of their income.

Lastly, based on how much you're contributing to an IRA, or 401(k), it's important to play around with the percentage of your pre-tax pay that you allocate to these programs in order to see what monthly net amount allows you to both invest intelligently in a retirement plan but also provides you with a bit of wiggle room with which you can pursue personal hobbies you love and afford the necessities of life. When you've nailed down this monthly figure, you can move onto prioritizing the activities that matter the most to you, as well as defining the necessities of your life.

Step 2: Figure out how much you're spending. By the time we've started our first foray into establishing a career, we've also most likely racked up a certain amount of subscription services. In the age of Netflix, Spotify, and related entertainment streaming applications, these types of recurring payments become a mainstay. One of the most valuable exercises when prioritizing what types of services to give your money to, is establishing your personal values. Would you rather have a gym service that costs $40 a month and forgo a media service, or instead opt to run outside each day for free, while having a couple of technology subscriptions? Of course, you might be able to afford both but that point is to answer the following question: What takes precedence for you? There are many values to consider like health, career, family, love, etc. Related services that align to these values might be spinning classes, furthering education courses, hosting a Sunday family dinner, or paying for a dating application.

Examining your current state in terms of voluntary expenses is also extremely important. You'll find that some of your biggest cost savings will be simply excising services that you're already paying for, but don't really utilize that much. For me, I had both a Hulu and Netflix subscription, and found that in the past month, I'd used Netflix 3 times, whereas family and friends who were bumming off my account had been using it 15+ times. Likewise, with Hulu, I figured out that I was only utilizing this $13.99 service for 2 shows that I watched religiously. Both shows were available for free on the cable provider's websites during the first week they aired. Additionally, I found, by analyzing my monthly tab that I had spent close to $40 at the movies. So, I swapped my Hulu and Netflix subscriptions for a MoviePass, and through these minor adjustments, that served my purposes much better than the previous arrangement, I was saving $60 per month, and $720 per year.

On top of voluntary desires, it's also important to examine your current necessities. Do you live in an expensive apartment? Are you living alone and could possibly share a two-bedroom with a coworker or friend? Would leasing a vehicle be more cost effective? Do you need cable service if you have a Smart TV and a Netflix subscription? Do you need a car at all if you only use it twice every six months to visit your parents out of state? These heavy hitter categories, if reduced, result in a much larger number to play with for investments, so adjusting them as much as possible, but ensuring that you're still comfortable and happy with your standard of living, is of utmost important.

Step 3: Factor in your annual costs. One of the biggest surprises I had during my first real year of budgeting was incurring annual costs. Your annual tax on your vehicle, or your annual car insurance payment (if you choose to pay it annually to save a bit of money) can end up being rude surprises that throw your entire budgeting projections out the window. For that reason, it's important to look back at your previous year's expenditures, and pinpoint annual costs that are bound to reoccur. Adding these one-time annual payments into any budgeting calculator that you end up using will save you a huge headache later in the year, and you won't be forced to scrape by with just $15 for outside eating per week for October - December, like I was!

Step 4: Create a monthly or annual pot for unexpected costs. 2008 Volvo S4, beautiful grey exterior, and leather grey seat interior. My dad bought it for me as a graduation gift, and it ended up being the most horrific car purchase of all time. All in all, that car cost and absorbed upwards of $12,000. A large percentage of this bill was in the form of unexpected costs that were incurred as a result of repeated services being needed for this car. It's difficult to totally avoid situations like this, and for this reason, you should set up a good amount of money on either a monthly or annual basis for "unexpected occurrences." Some years you will use all of it, and other years, you'll carry over a large chunk, regardless, it's important to have an emergency fund, a topic that's explored in further detail in a forthcoming chapter.

Step 5: Create goals for your monthly investment contributions. Finally, as far as expenditures go, it's important to delineate even, monthly contributions to your investments that reach an annual overall total goal that you're pleased with. Try to steer clear of setting vague goals like "Put more money into my 401(k)" and go towards "Put in $13,000 to my 401(k) this year". Track how much you contribute to these accounts on a monthly basis and ensure that you are maxing out any retirement funds, or at least are coming close to it.

For some, this calculation might be a simple equation of the amount of money you want to invest in a brokerage account, and dividing that into 12 equal parts. However, for others, who receive a bonus, or others who know they're going to receive a sizeable tax return, they might want to strategically positions larger payments around this time, and smaller payments everywhere else. It should be noted that this later strategy is riskier, as it's not a given that you'll receive a bonus, or that your annual tax return will be as large as it was in prior years.

Step 6: Choose the budgeting tool for you. There are thousands of budgeting tools to choose from. In fact, there must be at least a couple thousand that are just homemade excel files, made by budgeting enthusiasts. Many people prefer hand jamming their daily expenses into a sheet as such. However, it's important to note that with daily credit card swiping rates being in the double digits these days, personally inputting this information can be an extremely onerous task. Essentially, there are much more time efficient ways to proceed.

Though still working with excel spreadsheets, there are options that provide a worksheet where you input your monthly expenses by copying and pasting straight from your bank statement, after which you categorize each expense, and a live dashboard is updated on a separate worksheet. I know people that follow this path of budgeting and choose to look at is as a weekly reconciliation activity. However, there are even better and more refined ways to approach budgeting, especially since copy and paste functionality, as well as downloading .csv files, from banking websites can often be an unruly task due to the variety of pay periods different banks follow.

Automated applications like Mint provide a millennial style way for budgeting. You hook apps like these, of which there are many varieties, directly to your bank account, so all the expenses that funnel through you debit or credit cards are automatically displayed within the application. From this point on, you can categorize these expenses, as well as set category limits for each month. These apps usually allow for alerts when you're about to overspend, which helps with habit development. In reality, these apps work the same way as an excel sheet, but provide better trend analysis via built-in tools, as well as a much easier user interface. Some downsides of utilizing applications like these are security concerns with linking your banking accounts straight to a third-party application as well as a plethora of ads displayed in-app. It should be noted that these applications do not have to be linked to your bank account, and many people love them for the simple fact that they can load an expense in as soon as they make it by whipping out their smartphone. The ease of accessibility is definitely an advantage that mobile budgeting apps have over desktop applications or traditional spreadsheets.

As far as security is concerned with direct-link apps as such, full disclosure, this type of set-up is happening more and more (in applications like PayPal and Venmo), and while it does cause a certain degree of uneasiness, you should read up on user agreements and the security precautions they have in place. I'd be extremely hesitant to be a first-time user of a new application within this field, but I might be more willing to utilize one that's been in existence for a couple of years and doesn't have any reported security issues.

One option available to the security concerned amongst us is desktop budgeting applications like YNAB or Quicken. These applications largely do what an automated excel sheet would do, but allow for a more streamlined, user friendly interface, as well as much more built-in analytic features that will help you pinpoint bad habits. People tend to feel safer when an application is housed on the desktop, as opposed to on an online server. Additionally, these types of systems also allow for a direct link to your bank accounts, should you choose to utilize it, though many people prefer to individually migrate their expenses as an added security precaution. For people who don't like maintaining their budget in excel sheets, this is a great option, though it does usually cost quite a bit more than a well-developed macro-enabled budgeting workbook.

Step 7: Most importantly, stick with it!
Arguably the most important step of developing a budgeting system is sticking with it, month in, month out. At first, it might seem like a burden, counting up your pennies at the end of each day, week, or month. However, the first twelve months will be a great learning period, as you'll find out more about what expenses matter most to you, how to prioritize them, the different tools that you are utilizing most, and ultimately how to fit your expenses into your budget. One great tip that someone gave me soon after I'd started budgeting was to stop using my credit card for a month and instead switch over to cash. When you use cash, it's much more apparent how ridiculous a certain expense might be. Swiping for a $17 hat at an amusement park might be easy with your nagging nephew pulling on your leg, BUT you can just as easily push him aside when you realize how stupid you are for pulling one ten, one five, two one's, AND tax out for a hat he's only going to wear for six minutes. I wouldn't recommend doing this for more than a month or two because you're missing out on credit card benefits if you utilize this method for too

long, and additionally, carrying around a ton of cash probably isn't best practice.

Overall, with budgeting, you'll develop a much higher sense of self-discipline when it comes to your finances as you continue to practice this skill over time. Eventually, this skill will be something that will benefit not only your personal finances, but ultimately, every aspect of your life. Once you've followed and tweaked your plan over the course of a year or so, you'll have built a system that is easy for YOU to stick with. As your resolve grows, you'll be shocked when you reflect at just how easy it is for you to suggest activities like hiking (which is free) as opposed to going out for happy hour every day after work (which is not free).

<u>Key Takeaways</u>

- ✓ Create ***measurable*** savings goals, and track toward them! It's infinitely better to have a goal of saving a concrete 40% of your post-tax income per month, as opposed to having *a vague New Year's resolution of "saving more dough".*

- ✓ Though you might not realize it, developing <u>and sticking to</u> a budget is the fundamental requirement of reaching your loftiest goals. Figure out where you're leaking cash, analyze what you need and what you don't need, and **build priorities**! Do you really need that Hello Fresh subscription if half the food is spoiling because you're hopelessly lazy?

- ✓ **Don't be a rookie!** Factor in annual costs into your budget so you aren't blindsided with that May payment of $1,200 for your car insurance!

- ✓ Utilize a budgeting tool to become more mindful of every purchase you're making. Trust, it's harder to stomach a $11.48 ciabatta sandwich if you have to manually enter it in and see how it's *leaching away* at your $300 discretionary spending pot for the month.

Chapter 6:
Setting up an Emergency Fund

By far, one of the biggest pieces of advice that financial advisors will give to first-time investors is the necessity of devoting a large proportion of your leftover cash, month-to-month, to investment. Though I think that this is a great practice, and is one that should be adopted and made into more of an automated habit, I also believe that this is a *secondary* priority. By and large, the first priority for someone who is just starting to tackle their personal finances, is the establishment of a realistic emergency fund. The reason I think that it's important to discuss this issue is because many of the friends and coworkers that I've spoken to, have described to me that investing is more important than contributing to their emergency funds. In even scarier situations, I've known people who've pulled money from their emergency fund in order to invest! Of course, my buddies represent a very small part of the population, but as we can tell through surveys and reports, the relationship is pretty realistic in relation to society at large, as around 30% of Americans have absolutely no emergency savings!

One of the more dangerous outlooks I've seen in respect to emergency funds is the idea that credit cards can act as emergency savings. There's a ton of reasons why this logic is extremely flawed, and why this practice is particularly dangerous. First of all, there's the idea of interest. If you dump a major expense on your card, it could take you months to pay that off, and in the meantime, you'll have paid tons of money on interest payments. This consequence is a direct result of poor financial planning, because it's a situation that can be easily avoided. In addition, if you're new to personal finance, I'd think that your credit card minimum is low. So, whereas emergency funds force you to save out a realistically large amount of reserve cash, your credit card ceiling could probably not handle a catastrophic expense. This could possibly lead people with no other option but to take out multiple cards, and max them all out, creating a horrible situation. In addition, resorting to using your credit card, and then taking forever to pay if off, if ever, can lead to the development of both bad credit, as well as a future inability to take out cards, loans, and mortgages.

Now, I've described before one of my own, personal use cases for establishing an emergency fund, and the lessons I learned from not starting one early enough. Soon after I started my job as a teacher, I started to devote 100% of any left-over money that I had towards paying down my student loan debt. I was driven by the factor that I didn't want to experience any interest payments, in addition to the fact that most financial pundits tout the fact that paying down debt should be your first priority. However, as is the case with nearly everything in life, you need to be able to strike a balance. I learned the true gravity of this statement when my beloved Volvo, broke down seven months after I bought it. Suddenly, I was left with no transportation to get to work, and because I had not yet developed an emergency fund, I couldn't afford to get a new car at that point. This led to about a two-month period where I was bumming rides off my parents. Of course, this was a highly frustrating experience, but I did take a lesson from it, in that, regardless of whatever other costs I had in my life, contributing to my emergency fund was an absolute necessity. Though my "emergency" wasn't as pronounced as it is for others, one of the most common examples of why you'd need an emergency fund is to support yourself if you lost your job. Of course, other examples could range from a tree falling on the side of your home all the way to you developing a serious dental problem that requires a root canal or two; the possibilities are both random, and limitless!

How do I start developing an emergency fund? First and foremost, as is the case with all financial savings and planning, it's important to outline your personal goals. By developing an end goal of how much money you want in your emergency fund, along with how long you're going to give yourself to collect and save that, you'll be able to derive manageable monthly goals that you can easily fit into your budget. It's important to note that for most people just starting out, you'll likely have some loans, probably in the form of student loans. Therefore, it's important to strike some sort of balance between paying off your debts, along with contributing to your emergency fund. I would stress that at this time, your attention should be only on these two components, investment can wait until you've developed a fund that provides an adequate safety net for you.

One handy trick that I found was, within your annual budget, auto-excise your annual emergency fund goal. This forced me to both prioritize saving in my emergency fund, but it also made me accustomed to this reduced budget so I was able to adapt easily month after month. Had I had to make a conscious decision each month about how much I was going to contribute to my emergency fund, I can say, almost certainly, that I would've found excuses in certain months to contribute nothing.

How much should I save in my emergency fund? The question of how much, exactly, to save in one's emergency fund varies person by person. General advice is to save (3) months' worth of salary, so that if the worst happens, you can afford to support yourself in the immediate future. However, personally, I'd probably err on the side of caution, and save for (6) months' worth of salary. If you look at job hunting, holistically, you'll find most people take longer than three months to secure a job after being laid off. In this instance you can sort of appreciate the forward thinking that contributing to an emergency fund requires. When you have a job, and no issues have arisen, you're coasting, and you don't have any financial pressures on you. So, at that time, saving in an emergency fund might not seem like the biggest priority, because everything's fine. However, when things go south, financial pressures can put an insurmountable amount of pressure on a person, turning a bad situation into a horrible one, pretty fast. And, along those lines, it's impossible to predict if, when, or what you'll be using your emergency fund for, so saving (6) months' worth of salary provides a greater margin for security, and it's easy to do if you budget appropriately.

Where should I keep my emergency fund? A very important requirement of an emergency fund is the ability to have access to the reserves instantly, at any moment. Like people who resort to utilizing credit cards, others will often turn to retirement accounts in order to pay for emergency expenses, because they don't have an emergency fund set-up. We have described in detail how horrible it is to withdraw from a retirement fund in respect to the heavy taxes you'll incur, so this is not really a feasible or recommended option either. Likewise, investment capital can also take 2-3 days to entirely liquidate, based upon your broker. Because of the general inaccessibility of these types of accounts, it also poses an additional reason, if you needed one, to not look at them as some sort of cushion reserve, because getting money immediately isn't easily doable. Instead, storing an adequate amount in an emergency fund that you can easily liquidate is extremely important, and cannot be ignored if you simple "put money into your 401k".

Overall, it'd be in a person's best interest to keep their emergency fund in a high yield savings account. This allows for a marginal rate of return in the money that you store within this account, but at the same time, it enables you with the extremely important ability of being able to pull that money out when you need it most.

Key Takeaways

✓ **BEFORE** you rush into investment, realize the importance of developing a sound emergency fund!

✓ Never look at either your credit cards or your 401(k) as an emergency fund. This is both a dangerous and an irresponsible way of thinking about these funds. An emergency fund is a quickly accessible pot of real money that you can use in case the worst happens, it's not an excuse for you to max out your credit cards or start stripping money out of your retirement funds.

✓ Shoot for an emergency fund that has about *(6) month's worth of salary*, you want to provide yourself as much cushion as possible. IF the worst does happen, finances aren't something that should be your #1 concern.

✓ Stick your emergency fund in a place that *easily liquidated* like a high yield savings account. That money should be available to you in a moment's notice, that's what it's there for! Don't stick it in an investment account that will take upwards of a week to liquidate.

Chapter 7:
Investing Part I - Early Investing

How early should someone start investing? If someone had asked me this question five years ago, I would've said that I didn't know if I ever planned on investing. This was, of course, a very uneducated perspective on financial management and investing. You can't entirely blame me because in College, I was a science nerd that literally did not care about anything outside of my studies. In my insular cocoon, hidden deep in some chemistry lab that was decorated very 1980's, I wasn't filling my head with nonsensical thoughts of "money", instead I was learning about the structure of hemoglobin, duh! In all honestly, sure, I do wish I'd read up about all this stuff and had begun building a portfolio all those years ago. Now, years later, I have business school friends that have investments that are 7 years old, whereas my oldest investment is just 3 years old. This might seem like a nominal difference, but because of compound interest, the profit on those investments ends up being drastically different.

Understanding compound/simple interest is extremely important because they are the underlying factors within all investments. If you've been through grade school, and had an algebra course or two, you're probably familiar with the concept, memorized how to compute it, regurgitated formulas for exams, and then promptly threw this information out of your head. At the very basic level, an interest is something that is made by a lender, when he or she loans money to a borrower; a relationship in which the borrower provides the lender with interest as a part of the repayment. Now, there are two types of interest:

simple and compound. Within simple interest, things are, well, quite simple! Let's say your brother-in-law is starting a new company, and asks you to loan him some money so he can get his operation off of the ground. If he comes to you with the following terms, he's asking for an agreement based on simple interest: $20,000 today, with a repayment of the base plus 5% annual rate of interest paid annually over the course of five years. However, you could counter, and ask him for a 5% rate of interest, compounding monthly. Let's view the differences between these two arrangements, given a 5-year period of return:

Simple Interest
> **Initial Investment:** $20,000
> **Rate of Interest:** 5%
> **Return after Year 5:** $25,000

Compound Interest
> **Initial Investment:** $20,000
> **Rate of Interest:** 5%
> **Return after Year 5:** $25,667

You can see here, in this simple comparison, that compounding interest is the way to go, and it earns you more, but why? Well, when you have simple interest, you're only ever applying that amount on the principal, so in the case that we used, on $20,000. However, compounding interest acts as an "interest on the interest." This means that as the loan is paid, each month's compounding interest will include both the principal amount as well as any interest paid in prior periods. In this case, it ends with the lender earning $667 more than if we'd proceeded with a simple interest arrangement.

Now, if we take this example and extrapolate it over a much larger time, meaning a lot more money is invested, you'll see where the larger disparities come into play. In the example used, you'll have noticed that the relationship lasted for only five years. However, when you invest money in stocks, bonds, or retirement plans, you'll often be a part of these relationships for close to 20-40 years. The longer you benefit from that compound interest, the greater the possible benefits.

So, one can clearly see the issue of waiting to invest. If you decide to wait even five or ten years to start investing, you're shortening the period of investment drastically, and losing out on some serious cash! Plain and simple, people who wait even five years to get their investments underway will end up losing out on a sizeable amount of money. The same $25,000 invested when you're 25, as opposed to when you're 35, will end up producing nearly $135,000 more over the life of the investment (considering a 7% rate of return, and planned retirement at age 60).

Of course, other than just the increased rate of return you'll see over the years due to compound interest, there are definitely other reasons to start investing early! One of the biggest reasons is that the earlier you invest, the more time you'll have to make riskier moves, and the more the room you'll have for making any potential mistakes. Personally speaking, I made some horrible investment moves early on. The first of which was investing in technologies that I neither believed in, nor truly understood. I feel into a bad cycle of trusting "pundits" and online projection charts to direct my investments, which ended up being an extremely difficult lesson for me, and one that's still hard for me to swallow. But, I was young when I made those mistakes, and a couple of years on, I emerged with a reasonable loss, but a much more hardline education on the type of investments that were most worthwhile to me. Had I started my investment journey at 35, and made those mistakes then, I would've wasted even more valuable years, and had an added disadvantage to the one I already had, which was choosing to invest late.

Secondly, an often-overlooked reason to start investing early is because this is, in and of itself, a keystone habit: something that starts pouring over into every facet of your financial management life and encourages you to develop similar, beneficial habits. After I started investing, I finally started putting money aside to save, mainly because I wanted to be able to invest more than the $100 that I was putting in monthly. This in turn helped curb my affinity for expensive lunches, as mentioned in previous chapters, and forced me to finally develop a budget. I started to log all my purchases, and saw how to balance one day of overspending, with another day of doing less costly activities like utilizing free green space. Ultimately, my budgeting matured, and I started to put more of it aside at the beginning of the period after I had received my paycheck, live off a condensed budget, and totally avoid the habits of overspending that had plagued me in the past.

Finally, while it might be very hard to imagine right now, by investing early, you're saving yourself a ton of grief in the long run. By religiously putting money in your retirement accounts, like a 401(k) and a Roth IRA, you're setting yourself up for success later in life. Yes, it might seem an onerous task to devote a sizeable amount of your pre-tax dollars to a 401(k) right now, but you must realize that millions of Americans have zero savings by the time they retirement, and that could easily be you. If you desire to avoid an old age plagued by money concerns, or even worse, having to extend your working life to pay your bills, you must start putting your money to work NOW.

Additionally, not having enough saved at your projected age of retirement can possibly lead to a host of issues, some of which are financial. People who stay in the workplace longer are more prone to dealing with health issues brought on by stress and fatigue, all of which can cause increased health bills. It's difficult to imagine your life going down that route, but though it is painful to imagine this now, it will be many times more difficult to actually live that reality one day. Save yourself a ton of grief, and start putting money away into your retirement accounts as soon as you're financially able to.

While discussing retirement savings, it's also prudent to think of the source of your investment. Considering you begin your investment odyssey at a young age, it's a useful task to assess both your own reactions to certain stressful investment situations as well as to project out and think of important life events right around the corner. Speaking to the first point, for example, let's say you've backed a tech stock that tanks two weeks after you bought at (unknown at the time) an all-time high and has now fallen by nearly 15%, causing you to lose nearly $400. Will your first gut reaction be to sell? Will you obsess over it, checking the ticker price on the internet at all times of the day? In situations like this, it might be better for you to begin your investments with a 401(k) or IRA pre-tax contribution. This way, however much money you contribute, you're unable to touch it and all the trades conducted are done without much thought on your end. This way, you can let your investments sit without touching them much, and over the years, they will grow without the danger of you selling them off because you were uneasy during a short period of market volatility. Of course, at some point you are going to have to develop both the coping skills required to participate in a sometimes volatile market, as well as steadily improve your skills at choosing the right investment opportunities.

Now, speaking to the second point, since we are looking at this through the perspective of an early investor, it's important to note that there are various life events going on at the earlier stage of a young adult's life that are directly affected by the financial decisions they make. Marriages, education, and mortgages are only some of the things that demand a substantial financial contribution, and tend to take place in your early to late 20's. So, while maxing out a 401(k) may be a feasible feat for some, it might be a sheer impossibility for others. Simply saving for a down payment, which traditionally sits at 20%, can be a huge undertaking that requires a lot of cash on hand. For this reason, it's imperative that you find balance within your investment journey, and choose investments that will both allow for an unimpeded rate of growth, while at the same time, cater to the life events that you will need capital for. This might mean allocating more money to your savings at times, and curbing your 401(k) contributions, but doing personal research, as well as talking to a financial planner are required activities if you want to traverse this, often times complicated, landscape with good investment returns.

Overall, regardless of whether you're putting your money into a 401(k) plan, an IRA, mutual funds, ETFs, index funds, or even individual stocks, it's much more beneficial if you get started now, as opposed to waiting 10 years, at which point you'd be massively behind early investors. Always remember that if you wait, many more doors will be closed to you, but will be open to the others who decided to buckle down, budget, and invest early.

<u>Key Takeaways</u>

✓ Build a solid, foundational understanding of **WHY** compounding interest is so important, and why it is the primary reason why early investors fare better than those who wait to invest.

✓ Understand the implications of waiting to invest, this could land you YEARS <u>behind your peers</u> in terms of investment income.

✓ Don't overlook the powerful role that *sound habit formation will play in your life* – the sooner you start implementing responsible, consistent investment activities in your life, the faster it'll be to develop this into a lifelong habit.

✓ **<u>Learn to balance</u>** out your desire to invest, with your need to finance important life events, like having capital on hand to pay for a down payment, new car, or myriad other factors that pop-up in our twenties.

Chapter 8:
Investing Part II - Individual Stocks

If you've ever had a financial planning discussion with anyone in your life, ranging from your boss to you great-aunt Marilyn, they'll have likely give you the sage advice, "Make your money work for you." Cool, thanks, got it, but how? One of the best ways to go about this, as is touted in many different ways all throughout this book, is through investment. The one buzz word that most people associate with investment is often "stocks". Can I ask you a question? Do you know what a stock is? I'll be honest, I had no idea what a stock was when I first started my investment research. Yes, generally, all my life I knew they existed, but how someone bought one, made money off of it, or what it physically was remained a mystery for me. This isn't something to be ashamed of! I remember I used to be so self-conscious when trying to have a discussion with anyone about investment because I felt like a complete fake-o. The biggest part of learning sound financial investment techniques is building a good foundational knowledge of the investment world, and stocks are a great place to start.

The moment we've been waiting for...Stocks are pieces of a company, and when you buy one, you become a shareholder! For all intents and purposes, "stocks" and "shares" should be treated as synonymous words. Once you purchase a share, you now enter into an agreement where you've given your capital to this company to further its goals and missions. Essentially, you've provided them with a loan, and are now considered a shareholder within their company, an act for which you will, hopefully, be paid well for if the company continues to grow.

What does purchasing a stock entitle you to? But, not so fast! Just because you're considered a shareholder doesn't mean you're really entitled to anything other than the compound interest you'll receive over the years as you remain a loyal shareholder. Technically, yes, you own a piece of their company, but of course, it'd be idiotic to think that just because you bought a $5 stock, you have any say in their creative direction, the people they hire, or authority over their goods. It should be noted that this scenario, of purchasing a rather small part of a large company, is the case for the large majority of people. Rest assured that, essentially, you own nothing aside from that stock itself. If you want to read more about this concept of why you can't run out with a desk and chair from the Coca Cola Foundation after buying one of their stocks, read up on the concept of the Separation of Ownership and Control.

Now, there are definitely things that you DO get with buying a stock. For example, if you bought a voting share of a company, you can actually vote during their shareholder meetings! Most shares that you purchase through online brokerage portals are voting shares. To this end, every year Apple holds a Shareholder Meeting in Cupertino that you can get invited to, and it doesn't matter if the amount you own is as small as a single stock. Attendance at events like this is very sought after, and as a result, nabbing a spot on one of these meetings is up to chance. Still, very cool that you get invited!

Also, it's fair to say that the concept of purchasing a share to have voting rights in shareholder meetings is something that most people have seen played out in one form or another on TV.

Anyone remember the movie Au Pair? Disney Channel? Rom com about a MBA turned nanny who falls in love with the Fortune 500 CEO, whose children she's taking care of? Nope? Just me? Well, there are many more examples to source from within media which will make one familiar with the concept that owning a larger share of a company comes with a larger amount of power in voting decisions. So, if you buy up a ton of shares of a certain company, you have much more power in electing the board within that company, and the idea is they will vote and direct the company in accordance with your wishes. Of course, the vast majority of people never have to deal with voting rights and shareholder percentages.

Now, onto the discussion of how do I actually buy a share?! The first step towards buying a share of a company is doing your research. There are a multitude of resources online that will provide you the history of a particular company, and how it has performed since it began trading publicly within the stock market. The best advice I've ever received in regards to choosing which company to back is answering the age-old question of, "Do you know what this company does?" I could go online to a highly visited website right now and find (5) "hot stocks" that are involved in industries that I don't have the slightest clue about. It would be foolish of me to invest in these companies, because I do not have an accurate idea of how this market performs, or its future. However, if I decide to back a company that I am super passionate about, and understand a good amount about within the related industry, I'd feel both more comfortable and more confident about its future performance.

Following suit, one of the biggest factors that investors look into when researching a company is seeing if it pays out dividends as well as how the company's doing in relation to their finances (what's their debt situation? How much revenue growth do they see year over year?). Asking these questions and doing the personal research required to find the answers will help you avoid risk down the road. This was largely a lesson I learned the hard way! The first large order of share that I purchased was for a company that I did not believe in, but that had been performing well in the market. In fact, this company was touted as one of the "hottest companies to invest in" within a financial magazine that I'd been reading. So, based off the projections of a person I didn't know, and without any personal research, I put in a large order. Two months after I invested, it dipped tragically. That lesson burned me, for sure, but it taught me a ton as well, as now, regardless of the hype around a particular company, I refuse to invest in something that I do not understand or trust.

Now, once you've completed all that research, you can move onto establishing the prerequisites required prior to putting any orders in. First up is opening a brokerage account. Choosing your broker is a decision that you shouldn't take lightly, as it's largely going to be a long-lasting relationship, and one in which you'll be utilizing the same online interface so if you don't like it, it's going to be difficult for you to switch over at a later date. Avoid the hassle, and check out a couple of different options prior to committing to one broker. There are many websites online that rank these online brokers, but ones with low payments for trades are great like Charles Schwab or eTrade. After a day or two of transferring your funds, you can just point and click your way towards your first buy! Intimidating, and terrifyingly enough, all too easy.

Finally, one thing I must point out is that after you buy, don't become one of those freaks that checks your account every hour on the hour for changes. None of that crap matters and it ruins your quality of life when you train your mood to rise and fall with the market's ups and downs. In any given day, the value of your portfolio can fluctuate hundreds of times, so relax! It'd be best if you checked your account periodically, such as weekly, or better yet bi-weekly. This is not something to obsess over.

Explaining Order Types. One point that is important to discuss, and might be a point of confusion for the new investor, is order type. The basic type of order is a market order, which pushes the system to buy or sell your stock at the best current price. It's important to know that if you classify an order as a market order, it is executed immediately. I usually tend to stay away from market orders because they do not guarantee you a price, they only guarantee that you'll get what you asked for. For example, if you place a market order for 20 shares of a certain company, depending on how many market orders are in front of you, the price per share could vary dramatically as the market price of that share shifts. Market shifts are so volatile that from one second to the next, a share price could change so much that it causes your overall total to go up by a $100-1,000, depending on how much you bought. Essentially, you could end up paying much more than the price you decided on when you put that market order through.

The type of order I prefer is a limit order. With limit orders, you specify an upper limit price that you're willing to go to. So, when you put an order through, as long as your price meets that, or better, you'll buy shares. However, if the price of the share exceeds your limit, you won't get the entire fill you asked for. In my mind, I'm fine with that, because I do not want to overpay for any part of my order. When entering in your limit prices, try to set a limit that is right below the current price of the share if you're buying, that way you'll get around or better than the current market price.

Acting as the opposites to limit orders, stop orders are a way to confirm that the market is moving in the direction you want, prior to buying. To buy shares on a stop order, you set an amount after which the stop order becomes activated. Once this floor has been reached, your order is then converted into either a market or a limit order as discussed previously, a market order will cycle through, maybe fluctuate in price, and fill the entire order, whereas a limit order will fill until a ceiling is reached. A stop-limit order is obviously the better choice because it provides you with a higher degree of control over the price per share that you pay.

One of the last things to discuss when putting in an order is the duration. You'll be able to designate whether you want this order to go through the day, be executed at the open or close of the market for that day, proceed until a specific date, or set the time-out for a certain time, after which they are canceled. The variety of duration options you're provided allows you to play another angle, in which the broker portal watches the market and scoops items at the conditions you've set on either your limit or stop-limit order. Duration doesn't matter on a normal market order, as those are filled immediately.

What are dividends, and how do they benefit you? When talking stocks, it's important to discuss dividends. Dividends are profits that are distributed by a company to its shareholder on some sort of annual basis, like biannually or quarterly. When you're starting out, you'll probably receive very small dividends based upon your investment. For example, a large company might have it set that they distribute $10 per stock, so if you own 2 stocks, you'd only get $20, but if you own 2,000 stocks, you'd get $20,000.

Now, dividends are much better reinvested than kept, unless you receive a substantial amount of cash, and have an immediate need for it. Also, traditionally, retirees favor dividends because they offer a secondary source of passive income. Otherwise, it would be in your best interest to reinvest the dividends that you receive. Most online portals for buying and sell shares allow for options in which you automatically reinvest the dividends you receive. At many brokerages, these programs are called "DRIP - Dividend Reinvestment Programs" so consider enrolling in one of those. To note, some people might want to have a super close watch over every investment they make, and the issue with a DRIP is that your dividend will be utilized to buy a stock at perhaps an inflated price. You might not be happy with that, so that's a reason to stay away from a DRIP. Personally, I do not care that much, and generally trust the market to work out its kinks with the nominal dividends I currently receive. In addition, I'd rather the reinvestment happen automatically, rather than be an onus on me to reinvest, something that I could easily procrastinate on. If this procrastination was scaled out over months and years, I could potentially lose out on $10-30K in investments, which could get up costing me hundreds of thousands of dollars. Reinvesting your dividends is no joke!

In addition, it should be noted that dividends can be paid out as either stock dividends or cash dividends. In general, it's not awesome if the company is giving out a stock dividend because that means they don't have enough cash on hand to pay a cash dividend to its shareholders. Additionally, when they pay you out a stock dividend, that doesn't mean that the stock price remains the same, they adjust it based on the number of shares they dole out, meaning the stock price will be slightly deflated. However, I'm of the belief that receiving a stock dividend is much more valuable than receiving a cash dividend. There are definitive benefits to receiving a stock dividend in that it increases your shareholder value, and, you don't have to pay taxes on this value until you cash out. Additionally, the company is essentially giving you the option of cashing out whenever you want, in addition to giving you more value within the company. If you let your increased shares sit and accumulate, and the company ends up steadily doing well, this could mean a big payout for you in the future.

Lastly, when discussing dividends, it's important to note that not all companies pay dividends. This is because of a multitude of reasons. First off, growing companies usually choose not to pay out a dividend because they're rapidly expanding and need to invest capital on their growth. Other companies, that might be well established, still choose not to give out dividends because they want to reinvest everything back into the company. If you really want to develop an additional income stream via dividends, you should do research into which stocks give out solid, consistent dividends.

Investigating the various types of stock. The two main stock types are common stock and preferred stock. A preferred stock is more like an agreement of terms throughout the life of a relationship, whereas common stock is a bit more fluid. Common stock, as described in this chapter, is a share that allows you voting power, sometimes might provide a dividend, though the amount of this dividend varies. Preferred stock has a pre-agreed amount of dividend, and provides no voting rights. Now, again, the voting part isn't my biggest concern, but the fact that if I agree to a stunted divided today, and the company does amazingly in the future, I could end up getting less of dividend than common stockholders, as my agreement cannot change, bothers me. At the time of investment, the dividends being paid out by preferred stock seem to be much bigger than the common stock variety, but, keep in mind that times change, and one day the common stock dividend could overtake the preferred stock dividend. Many people out there prefer to invest in a bunch of different preferred stock, and take a passive income in dividends. Personally, if you don't have a huge portfolio, and are just starting out, I'd stick with common stocks.

But, are there downfalls to investing in individual stocks? Yes, definitely! Starting out with one of the most daunting downfalls of investing in individual stocks - it's that the onus of building your personal portfolio falls to you. Whereas with other investment options, shares are bundled together in packages, making it much easier to pick a strong, diversified "horse", individual stocks are tricky, and require a ton more personal research and dedication. Of course, some of us are naturally more inclined to conducting personal research and being highly invested in our financial decisions. However, even with this subset of people, it's important to note that people who've based their entire careers on the market, like analysts, should be the ones conducting this research, likely not you, me, or Joe down the street.

Lastly, there are a ton of dangers if you don't diversify your portfolio correctly. For example, if you put a large majority of your capital behind just (4) individual horses, and a PR scandal happened to entirely kill off one of them, this is an incredible blow to the health of your overall portfolio. Whereas, if this capital was spread out over 30-40+ stocks, wrapped up in different entities, the blow would be miniscule, if felt at all. So, while having a couple of shares in a strong blue-chip stock, a company that has revenue in the billions, is a good idea, matching that with a more diversified portfolio of mutual funds, ETFs, index funds, and even commodities is MUCH more favorable than just investing $100,000 in Facebook, Apple, Netflix, and Toyota.

<u>Key Takeaways</u>

✓ A stock and a share are **synonymous** terms where you're buying a piece of a company. Don't get too excited. A single share of Apple doesn't give you enough <u>street cred</u> to call yourself a majority owner, buying a small amount entitles you largely to the compound interest alone.

✓ Buying a stock does **NOT** start with www.hotstocktips.com, rather, it starts with dedicated research that'll end up saving you on so much monetary pain later.

✓ Along those lines, research brokerages, pick the best one, and **<u>UNDERSTAND</u>** how order types can save you from "hidden" fees.

✓ Dividends are cool! If you're *super risk averse*, trying to just set up a passive source of income, or close to retirement, investing in large dividend bearing stocks might be the bet for you.

Chapter 9:
Investing Part III - Mutual Funds

I've mentioned diversification a million times by now, so let's discuss just how I began diversifying my OWN portfolio. The first foray I had into diversification, after I made horrible moves by buying bogus individual stocks without conducting any prior research (power move), was by starting to invest in mutual funds. So, let's keep it real, when I was just starting out, I found investing to be very complicated. Every stage was a hurdle, from choosing a broker to putting an order in, it seemed that every component had a hundred different steps that I had to understand. Added on top of that complication was seeing that my portfolio hadn't done as well as I had intended, because I never put any time and energy into doing any personal research.

Essentially, when I finally got to the stage where I was ready to start purchasing shares of a company, I automatically assumed that these shares would be individual stocks, and that this was the only option. My naiveté in the world of investing had me believing that everyone out there was just buying individual shares from a single company, and building their portfolio that way. So, I started buying shares from individual companies, and saw how putting all your eggs in one basket is a recipe for disaster!

In particular, my investments suffered because I put about 80% of my working capital behind a technology company that had a huge PR scandal. This caused their market price to dip 20%, and I saw my hard-earned cash literally disappear overnight. Now, in this case, I did not panic sell, even though I really, desperately wanted to. I hung onto the investment, and a couple of years later, I finally got back to the price that I'd originally paid, after which I did decide to sell, and reinvest that money into a mutual fund whose management I believed in. That single investment in the mutual fund has appreciated 40% in the past quarter, whereas my initial investment in the technology company didn't make me any money whatsoever.

So, while I do recommend that if you truly believe in a company, and have studied both the future products or services it plans to roll out, as well as its recent revenue growth, you should go ahead and purchase shares from a single company, I'd highly suggest going for a more diversified option. I'm not saying that you shouldn't buy shares from individual companies, I still do that today. What I am saying is that to truly achieve balance and diversification within your portfolio, you should include a variety of investment types. This allows you to have the greatest potential reward, and avoid the risks associated with a low level of diversification.

So, what is a mutual fund? A mutual fund is a company in and of itself, so, you can't "purchase" a mutual fund, but you can invest in it. When you start out by investing in a mutual fund, which can be done through all the popular brokerages, you'll put down an order that will act as an investment within this company. The mutual fund then pools all the money from its lenders and starts investing this capital in a highly diversified set of stocks, providing their lenders with the earnings.

How do I purchase a mutual fund? Mutual funds can be purchased either through the fund manager (Vanguard, T. Rowe, etc.) OR you can purchase them through your broker. It should be noted that mutual funds are a bit different from stocks in that they don't require an order type. You simply invest a certain amount of money, and it's filled. There is disparity present in the amount needed to invest, as some funds require you to put in a minimum order that would be considered high, whereas others offer lower buy-in amounts. Overall however, this isn't something to be particularly concerned about, as there are many strong funds that have an accessible buy-in amount.

The Human Factor. Now, depending upon the mutual fund that you choose to lend your money to, it's going to be managed by a totally different group of people. So, going into mutual fund investment, you should be aware of the people factor. All the trades of stocks, bonds, and other related investments are going to be controlled by humans, who are aided by machines, but can commit very human mistakes! There is a risk, and you should be aware of it. However, you should understand that the people in control of that fund are experts in the field, and that this is their full-time job, to look after YOUR investment. Overall, that risk is balanced out by a great reward, and there are multiple factors that make mutual fund investment an attractive one.

The Diversification Factor. One fact about mutual funds that really drew me in is that with one investment in a mutual fund, I could invest in a portfolio that had within it the 500 top companies within the United States of America. Now, if one of these 500 companies went south, or even 10 of them, it would affect my investment, but wouldn't impact me even a fraction as horribly as if I'd invest all my money amongst shares within those companies. That added cushion, when your money is spread out over multiple well performing companies, is something that's a huge plus to investors.

The Money Factor. Mutual Funds aren't terribly expensive, so to be able to allocate your $250 investment towards a fund that holds shares across 500 companies is a massive reward for a small tab. Now, if you started out with that same $250 and tried to build a diversified portfolio through purchasing of shares from individual companies, it'd likely be impossible. To build a truly diversified portfolio, you'd have to have a stake in at least 10 different companies, and with brokerage fees per transaction considered, it'd be extremely difficult for you to build a strong portfolio with a small cash start. So, in this case, the option of mutual funds is an obvious, and strong choice.

The Time Factor. Mutual Funds don't require a huge amount of time commitment from the investor at all. Because they are so closely managed by the portfolio managers at these large companies, this is largely a hands-off investment on the part of the investor. Whereas when you personally build your own portfolio, which requires a strong eye and a guard dog type mentality, to monitor any fluctuations in the small number of companies you're invested in, mutual funds are so diversified, and already so closely monitored, that you can be hands off with them. In fact, I often feel stronger about security with my mutual fund investments because professionals, whose entire job is to watch the health of the portfolio, are watching these investments, whereas the personal investments I've made in individual companies are all on me.

However, as with all things, with the good, comes the bad. There are definitive downsides to mutual funds that a new investor should be aware of. First and foremost, mutual funds are not traded on the stock market. Though you can purchase them through your brokerage, when you purchase them you interact with the fund, and not with the exchange. The mutual fund investments you make do not behave like a stock, and instead, they trade once a day, at the close of the market. This is an issue for people who'd like their trades to react to real-time market fluctuations.

Perhaps one of the biggest things that draws people away from mutual funds is market performance. In general, mutual funds perform more poorly than indices, a topic we will discuss in a forthcoming chapter. These performance issues can be linked directly back to the fact that in the end of the day, these funds are managed by people. In addition to human mistakes, the people factor also contributes to the fact that there are often hidden management fees that these mutual funds will charge you. Because these funds are huge companies, they have an equally huge payroll, with accountants, analysts, you name it, and though investment profit pays for most of that bill, you will also be contributing to that tab. And finally, one of the biggest issues that I wrestled with was the concept of cash. Because there are so many investors within a mutual fund, the fund must keep a large amount of its money on cash so that they're able to pay off investors who choose to withdraw. However, as we all know, cash sitting on the table is not generating interest, or income, for anyone, and that's a huge deterrent for people.

Overall, I believe that mutual funds are a more advantageous first-time investment for the newbie investor, as opposed to investing in individual stocks. As a young investor, you'll start out with a small amount of money, with which you can purchase a very diversified portfolio via mutual funds. As you continue your education about investing, you can rest assured that you first step in investing was likely not a misstep. Of course, as your knowledge about the market increases, it's recommended that you start to diversify your portfolio by doing the research required to safely invest with an individual stock. Essentially, don't fall for the idiot's trap and read all these finance magazines that give you targeted advice. Just because a website says that a gold company in Dublin has a rocketing share price doesn't mean that you should invest in it, because you likely have no idea about the Irish economy, or that market in particular. In the end of the day, speaking personally, I wish I'd invested in a strong mutual fund as opposed to the one-off Technology Company that caused me to lose big! Starting, out, unequivocally, a smarter decision would be to get involved with fund investment as opposed to haphazardly dumping all your money into companies and industries that you most likely don't have a clear understanding of.

<u>Key Takeaways</u>

✓ ***Diversify, Diversify, Diversify!*** Investing in individual stocks alone is NOT the move. Start investing in types of investments that might not be as familiar to you, like mutual funds.

✓ Unlike stocks, when you invest in a mutual fund, you <u>don't</u> buy a share of that company, instead you invest an amount of money that is then reinvested in a diversified portfolio set-up by the fund.

✓ It's easy to understand the pros of a mutual fund. When you invest $500 in 5 stocks of a company, you're in with that company alone. When you invest $500 in a mutual fund, that money is allocated over hundreds of companies, meaning **lower risk**, and **potentially higher reward**.

✓ Learn to love passive investment as a <u>newbie</u> investor. Yes, a team of professional financial analysts managing your fund for you is a **GOOD** thing.

Chapter 10:
Investing Part IV - ETFs

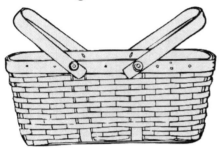

Another popular avenue for investment that an early investor should consider is the Exchange-Traded Fund (ETF). ETFs can kind of be considered as the third cousin twice removed of the mutual fund. Though these two share quite a bit of DNA, they're pretty different in how they behave. In particular, it's important to understand ETFs because, for a variety of reasons, an investor might prefer an ETF over a mutual fund, and understanding the pros and cons associated with picking one over the other will help an investor make a more informed decision. First and foremost, at the basic level, one very attractive quality that they both share is that ETFs too are a basket of assets, meaning that they provide a great deal of diversification, just like mutual funds do. And, just like mutual funds, an ETF is a fund that sells off ownership of the assets it owns, but in this case, ETFs are sold by converting the whole pie into shares. After these points of similarity, however, the two diverge on a host of key qualities.

Public Stock Market. Unlike a mutual fund, partial ownership of which you wouldn't purchase on the public stock market, an ETF acts just like a normal stock, and is traded and purchased similarly. This is seen as the great benefit of an ETF, as it mimics normal stock behavior and trades throughout the day, as opposed to mutual funds, which only trade once a day (after the market has closed). Because of this distinction, investors who want their money to respond to real time fluctuations in the market often prefer to proceed with ETFs as opposed to mutual funds.

Purchasing an ETF. Buying an ETF is very similar to buying an individual stock. Unlike mutual funds, in which you can place any amount of investment capital (based on the minimum required to buy in), purchasing an ETF requires an analysis of the share price. If one share costs $25, you will only be able to execute an order for (4) shares if you have $115, essentially, that extra $15 cannot be utilized to purchase part of a share, as shares are purchased whole. Whereas, in a mutual fund, you can invest any dollar amount without having to calculate share price.

Similarly, all the order types we discussed earlier (Market, Limit, Stop, etc.) are also applicable to ETF orders. Of course, as is the case with purchasing individual stocks or mutual funds, it's helpful to look at the past performance of an ETF prior to purchasing, though this is of course not indicative of any future boons. Personally, as an investor, I like to see a strong trend analysis that shows that this particular fund has stood the test of time. But of course, you must take into consideration the reality that the market is volatile, and these historic trends could mean nothing if a catastrophic market event happens tomorrow. But, for the most part, it is very helpful to look at these trends when investing in a fund because it gives you a taste of how well these portfolio managers perform over time, as well as a loose idea of how this investment will perform in the future.

Management of an ETF. When you consider the topic of ETF management, you realize that, essentially, there is none - and that this is a plus for some investors! Unlike the mutual fund, ETFs attempt to mimic the performance of a specific index they are targeting, a concept that we will discuss in detail in the following chapter. Because the ETF is attempting to mimic this target, it can be managed much, much more passively than the traditional mutual fund, which is adjusted daily by a large portfolio management team. Many investors prefer index mimicking because, when that index is performing well, their ETF performs well, too. In addition, there are a good number of investors out there that are just plain skeptical of portfolio management by humans, so in and of itself, they prefer that the portfolio be as passively managed as possible.

However, this concept brings a defining issue that was important for me to understand, prior to deciding whether I'd like to put more of my capital behind a mutual fund, or an ETF. Because there are administrative costs associated with an ETF, as there are with mutual funds, the ETF will not post as high as the index it's tracking, so when you see slightly depressed values, that's normal, because you're pulling the administrative costs out of that gross profit. At first, the fact that the ETF wasn't tracking exactly to the index and posting identical numbers was a point of confusion for me, but considering administrative fees, I saw the slight lag. This is an issue that's made further irrelevant because of the passive management involved with an ETF, the administrative costs associated with it will be significantly lower than what you'd typically see with a mutual fund.

Tax Benefits. The issue of taxation on mutual funds vs ETFs can get a bit hairy, but understanding the pros and cons behind it can end up saving you some serious cash. Essentially, it comes down to one factor: the portfolio turnover rate. When you buy or sell a security, your turnover rate increases. As a rule, mutual funds have a much higher turnover rate than ETFs. Because of the higher turnover rate, the mutual fund is creating many more instances of taxable events, whereas an ETF is designed to largely avoid these. With mutual funds selling and buying securities left and right, they sometimes realize a capital gain based on the timeline of the purchase. We discuss taxation in detail in a forthcoming chapter, but what that really means it that when a mutual fund sells off an asset before a year is up, which is a scenario they try to avoid, but happens quite regularly, there's an added tax that is sent to you, even though you might not have made money off that sale. However, since the mutual fund sold the security prematurely, and you're an "owner" in that fund, that is seen as a capital gain in respect to your personal taxes. And so, when this capital gain is passed onto the shareholders, a taxable event occurs because of that physical liquidation of assets. However, with an ETF, you're just trading on an exchange, and no liquidation is occurring, which makes the whole process much more tax efficient because much fewer of these "taxable events" occur.

Commissions. Unlike mutual funds, in which you don't have to pay any commission to invest, ETFs do charge a nominal commission on purchase. This fact can either mean a lot to you, or not matter at all. If you are investing large sums of money only a couple of times, then a $5 commission fee isn't going to kill you. However, if you are investing $100 a week, those commission fees will add up, and might eclipse the administrative costs of mutual funds. So, devising a strategy to either save and invest strategically, or think of shifting to a broker that offers commission-free ETF purchases would be smart. Of course, I wouldn't recommend picking a broker JUST because they have commission-free ETF purchases, but it's one of a multitude of factors that you should consider when making an informed decision.

What's better for me? Choosing between an ETF and a mutual fund can be difficult, as they both bring distinct, attractive qualities to the table. But I'd say, why do you have to choose one or the other? If your end goal is to diversify your holdings, you should hold investments in both strong mutual fund, as well as strong ETFs. For the smart investor, investing in either will be extremely beneficial in the long-run. Starting out, I'd recommend investing in a strong ETF and a strong Mutual Fund. The great things about both types of investments is that they are easily accessible, even to those with very little cash, and offer you a very diversified portfolio with which to begin your investment journey.

Key Takeaways

✓ An ETF is pretty similar to a mutual fund, in that it's a *huge ole' basket of assets*. BUT ETFs are neatly packaged into stocks, whereas mutual funds are not.

✓ ETFs are cool in that they're even **more passive** than mutual funds, meaning lower admin costs. They track an index, and because there's not as much brain power going towards tracking, they have less overhead than a mutual fund.

✓ **Tax attack.** It's true. The dark dark secret of mutual funds is that they create taxable events due to turnover. ETFs are traded on an exchange, so YOU oversee selling/possibly incurring tax due to a premature sell.

✓ TL;DR - Mutual Funds AND ETFs are beneficial. Remember...**DIVERSIFICATION** is the name of the game! You can have your pie and eat it too.

Chapter 11:
Investing Part V - Index Funds

So, there's a subset of grandpas out there that will have you believing that investing in anything other than something known as an Index Fund is sheer stupidity. I have interacted with said grandpas. While I don't see their illogical approach to diversification, and know for a fact that most of them invest in individual shares of Amazon, thereby negating their blah blah blah altogether, I'll give them an ounce of credit and affirm the importance of index funds. Really though - other than your own dad, taking stock tips from people who wear dad hats, whether they be the 20-year-old crypto aficionado, or a random old guy you meet at a family picnic is NOT a good idea.

Now, we've discussed both mutual funds and ETF's, so we can start talking about a third type of investment that can be packaged as either a mutual fund or an ETF, but has its own set of distinct characteristics - an Index Fund. An Index Fund, as the name implies, has one sole purpose, to track an index. To completely understand what an Index Fund does, it's important first to grasp what an index is. Once you've formed a good foundational knowledge of this type of fund choice, there will be a short discussion on how to invest in Index Funds, and whether it's a preferable choice over a traditional Mutual Fund, ETF, or simply investing in individual stocks.

What is an Index? When thinking of an index, relate it back to when you were studying for an exam and used an index card. After reading a 40-page chapter, you condensed this information onto 10-15 index cards, with each card representing a set of information from a subset within that chapter. Like that overall chapter, the stock market is huge, so tracking every single security would be an extremely difficult task. To condense this information, a sample size is taken called an index. This index is composed of a set number of stocks and represents a portfolio in and of itself. By utilizing the health of that index, you're able to track a subset of the stock market that you're interested in knowing more about, or tracking for your own investments.

In exploring exactly how an index is utilized, it's also important to note that if you see a certain growth rate within the index, it's assumed that this growth is happening proportionally in every stock within that index. The way this growth is calculated is by using a sophisticated weighting technique that takes into consideration the size and market value of all the stocks within an index and calculating a corresponding price. Also, while it is possible for anyone to create an index, because it's literally just a collection of stocks, for investing purposes, the ones created by powerhouse financial institutions are likely the ones that will benefit you most.

What is an Index Fund? An Index Fund is a fund, either a Mutual Fund or an ETF that tries to mimic an established Index. Because the work they're trying to do is essentially copy a pre-existing Index, most of these index funds choose to follow suit after the strongest Index Funds in existence, namely the S&P 500. Most investors do have a keen interest in investing in the S&P 500, so understanding what it is important. S&P 500 stands for "Standard & Poor's", and it's an index fund that is very closely assembled to include the top 500 American companies that trade publicly on the stock market. This index in particular is so popular because it constitutes a large part of the market as a whole, and thus, mimics the overall performance of it as accurately as is currently possible. So, in most cases, when you do invest in an index fund, the index fund will most likely be tracking the S&P 500.

Should I choose an actively managed fund or an Index Fund? First and foremost, if you're reading investment articles in Kiplinger or Money magazine, you'll find at least one article sprinkled in there about how Index Funds are preferable to Mutual Funds because historically, they almost always outperform them. But, at the same time, most investors are also cognizant of the fact that one of the biggest draws about a managed fund, like a traditional mutual fund, is the chance that it will outperform the market. A lot of people think that they shouldn't be relegated to just getting the market return, and that if they pick the right team, a managed fund could outperform an index fund. Evidence for that is lacking, as index funds do truly outperform mutual funds in most cases. However, from 1997-2007, 16% of actively managed funds did truly outperform their index, so taking that into consideration is important.

With all things, there is the discussion of how much it will end up costing you to invest. With an actively managed mutual fund, administrative fees can rack up, and taxes can also cut down severely on your overall profits. With Index Funds, since they are passively managed, the administrative costs are comparatively lower, which is also one of the big reasons that Index Funds outperform actively managed mutual funds on a regular basis.

How can I invest in an Index Fund? Thankfully, we live in the age of online brokerages! You can invest in an index fund just like you purchase stocks online, through an online brokerage portal.

Depending on whether the index fund you're most interested in is a mutual fund or an ETF, you'll have to proceed differently, but both transactions can be made in the same brokerage portal. It should be noted that the amount of money you need to access index fund investing is low, making this a very accessible investment. If you're limited on your cash, make it a point to research cheaper index funds, and make sure that their stock to bond ratio, as well as the index that they track, align with your comfort zone and interests.

Should I invest in an international index fund? As we've discussed, the most popular index funds are those that are associated with tracking the performance of American companies, like the S&P 500. However, there are strong index funds set up that track indices that include International Companies. Some of the most popular international index funds that people invest in are situated in Japan, Europe, and in a growing rate, Africa. Educating yourself on the growth of the economies in these countries can be daunting enough for people to forgo investing in international index funds, stocks, or mutual funds, but I believe that this is still a great way to diversify your portfolio even more.

Are Index Funds better than Mutual Funds, ETFs, and individual stocks? This is another question in which it'd be nonsensical to say that you should ONLY invest in Index Funds. There are definitely risk averse people out there that will give you pointed advice that you should only invest in index funds. Obviously, that's severely limiting the amount of diversification you could potentially create within your portfolio, and thus making it weaker. It's funny how often these questions are asked as well, because younger investors are coming from the mindset that they must choose just one option, when obviously, that's not true. To build a truly diversified portfolio, it's imperative that you invest in a variety of different investment streams, ranging from actively managed mutual funds that you believe might outperform the market, to S&P Index Funds that are generally embraced by most.

Key Takeaways

✓ Index Funds are funds that track the performance of an "index" of the public stock market. They basically aim to track or **mimic** the performance of a bunch of stocks.

✓ S&P 500 is a <u>HUGELY</u> popular index fund, because it tracks the 500 most successful companies in the domestic U.S.

✓ Catch-22. Index funds can be **ETFs OR Mutual Funds** - so purchasing them will vary based on the type of Index Fund you pick.

✓ There's literally <u>THOUASNDS</u> Of Index Funds out there. There's some that focus on technology, others that focus on international markets like Japan - I'm a fan of investing in a diversified set of varied Index Funds, pick up something in XYZ market if you feel that market is booming, *don't just limit yourself to S&P 500.*

Chapter 12:
Investing Part VI - Commodities

Commodities are an interesting topic within investment because you'll meet people that vehemently oppose going near them, but then you'll meet others who see them as just another positive means to creating a more diversified portfolio. There is a clear-cut distinction as to how a commodity differs from a normal stock, based primarily in the type of good being traded. By definition, a commodity is essentially a natural good or raw material. Examples of commodities range from oil, which is an extremely popular commodity to invest in, to plain ole apple juice. Most likely, if you've invested in a mutual fund, ETF, or Index Fund, you could very well already be involved with commodities trading and not know it, because you're not aware that the portfolio already contains commodities. As is with all vehicles of investment, one should know the downsides and upsides of investing in commodities, as well as know the safest and smartest ways to invest.

Upsides of investing in commodities. I am a glass half full type of person, so we'll begin with a discussion of why commodity investing is a recommended avenue to explore. Overall, the nature of a commodity can kind of be explained in one short correlation: when your stocks are doing well, your commodities are doing poorly, and vice versa. Yes, this is a very simplistic explanation, and it should be noted that because of the general volatility of the commodity market, which is known to be extremely volatile, this hard and fast rule does not always hold true. However, this rule has played out in reality many times in the past, and when it does, the investors who've taken advantage of commodities, end up doing very well in comparison to those who didn't. The underpinnings of this relationship are based on inflation. When the economy is experiencing a high rate of inflation, the stock market suffers, but under these same pressures, commodities end up doing pretty well. That's pretty self-explanatory because with inflation going up, services cost more, so basic commodities can get away with charging more for the good. So, with this logic, one can deduce that when inflation starts to rise within the economy, which it invariably will at one or more points in your investing life, you'll have a cushion that normal investors won't. So, whereas mostly everyone else who did not invest in commodities will see a dip in their portfolio, your own dip will not be as drastic if you offset appropriately with commodities.

Now, one characteristic of the commodity market is both a plus and a minus, depending on which side of the equation you fall on. Commodity markets are EXTREMELY volatile, meaning they see huge differences in price that is largely based off factors that most people cannot see coming, and thus, adequately prepare for. For example, issues in government relations can directly affect the price of oil and cause it to skyrocket overnight, ultimately benefiting the investor. Likewise, embargoes and termination of treaties can cause random commodities to have a huge dip in price. It should be noted that over the past decade or so, commodity prices have been generally rising as the overall world population has increased, while at the same time, resources have continued to dwindle. In addition to this difference amongst commodities and stock, there is another reason why they differ so greatly. If you have a bunch of different semiconductor companies, these companies are basically selling the same product, but based upon the strength of their product, their share price will vary greatly. However, commodities, like wheat, are usually packaged at the same price regardless of how they're being sold, because there's generally zero variability in the product.

Admittedly one of the biggest draws of commodities is the ability to hedge. Commodities aren't sold like normal stocks, in that they aren't sold for a current price. Instead, when one gets involved in commodities, they enter into a futures contract, in which they agree to buy or sell commodities at a future time and price. This is risky, very risky, but if you hedge correctly, meaning you take a long position, in which you sell you commodities, or take a short position, in which you buy them, you're taking a stance on the direction that you think the market is headed, and intending to profit from it. Hedging a commodity is difficult and risky, but it can definitely pay off if you've studied the market appropriately. Would I recommend it for a newbie investor? Heck no! I probably wouldn't even recommend it to a person who's proven to be a strong investor, based off the fact that hedging commodities just doesn't fall under the purview of a normal investor. Instead, I'd probably recommend investors to search for an avenue of passive commodity investment, where these hedging decisions can be left to excerpts, like Bill Ackman.

Lastly, while commodities are usually volatile, there is an added benefit in that they can't really be manipulated. Because these commodities are controlled by various government entities, and represent an actual raw good, it's much more difficult to price rig them than it is a normal stock from Company XYZ. This adds a bit of security for people who put their money down on commodities, hoping that going forward, if people are willing to pay more for it, there is an added cushion in that the price can't be manipulated to the extent that it can be for a normal stock.

Downsides of investing in commodities. One of the biggest drawbacks of investing in commodities is that they don't make you any money while they're sitting there. Commodities do not provide any interest or dividend payments to their investors. Instead, during the time you're holding onto that commodity, you'll largely be paying maintenance fees, and not making a single dime until you decide to sell at the correct time. Added to that issue is the fact that many people are skeptical of the individual ability to be able to forecast correctly, meaning that commodities investment spell out a recipe for disaster for most people. Individuals who don't have the patience, or honestly the drive to conduct personal research, end up losing massive amounts of money on trades. In all honestly, even though I do believe commodity investing can add diversification and value to your portfolio, entering into a futures contract as an individual and actively investing in commodities as a newb is a great way to lose your money! However, with that being said, there are passive ways of investing in commodities that will provide you will all the benefits associated with commodity investing, while leaving the difficult choices to trained experts.

How to Invest in Commodities. There are two ways to go about commodity investing. One way, which I think is above the paygrade of someone just starting out in investing, and honestly an approach that I will likely never utilize, and then there's another that is safe, and a wonderful way to diversify your portfolio. So, let's begin with the risky! A Futures Contract is an agreement that investors enter when purchasing a single commodity. Now, there's a ton of downsides to this, first and foremost, you need a crap ton of cash, something in the $10,000's range, to get started. Additionally, you are now the custodian of this natural resource, and managing that can, in certain situations, fall to you. So, because of the inaccessibility paired with its complicated nature, I would never advise anyone to enter into a Futures Contract as an individual investor.

Now, the more preferred way of investing in commodities is investing in an ETF that includes commodities. Because ETFs are traded on the regular stock market exchange, and don't require an enormous amount of money to access, this option is by far the preferred starting point for someone who has a growing interest in commodities, and there's even ETF's that go as far as specializing in commodities alone. ETF's that specialize in commodities behave quite similarly to ETF's in general, in that they work to track a specific industry. As with all ETF's, that track is never certain, and, because of the volatility of the commodity market, the tracking can be worse for commodities than for an ETF that tracks an index the normal stock market. Overall, as we've pointed out, ETF's are a smart way to diversify your portfolio, because they require a small amount of cash, alleviate risk should an inflationary environment arise during your investment journey, and still provide you with access to commodities, which are generally difficult to access as an individual investor.

Key Takeaways

✓ A commodity is an agricultural product or a natural resource, so they constitute anything from crude oil to mango juice! (Not Maaza though, that stuff is fake).

✓ Commodities **GENERALLY** play out opposite to the public stock market. I want to stick a huge asterisk next to this statement because it is NOT a hard and fast rule. But, to avoid risk if the market turns, many people take on commodities, that will most likely ease the financial burden.

✓ Why is that? Law of Supply & Demand! Recession = inflation = HIGHER prices for basic goods, meaning commodities do well, while the stock market suffers.

✓ Buying commodities CAN be done through a Futures Contract but you are **NOT** daddy Warbucks so please, stick to ETFs that specialize in commodity investment if you want to get involved with them.

Chapter 13:
Investing Part VII - Bonds

In any discussion of investment, two basic concepts that everyone should understand is the idea of a stock and of a bond. We've discussed a stock, which is essentially a part of a company that you buy to receive earnings as that company grows. Bonds work on a similar monetary premise, but their intended purpose is quite different. Unlike a stock, bonds don't entitle you to any ownership, but rather, they act as a plain old loan. One of the prevailing reasons why understanding bonds is so important to the newbie investor is because, usually, when you open a 401(k) account, IRA, or other passively managed investment account, the parameters for investment that you will provide the broker with are the ratios of stocks and bonds you want your portfolio to be made up of. Thus, understanding what a bond is, and furthermore, understanding what the ideal allocation of stocks and bonds within your portfolio should be, is very important.

What is a bond? The best way to succinctly explain a bond is to say that, well, it's basically a loan. Usually, when people think "loan", it's automatically attached to the idea of a banking institution providing an individual person a loan. The loan arrangement in regards to bonds is a bit different in that an individual person can purchase a bond, and now be lender to a huge corporation, or even the government! The incentive of private corporations or the government to issue these bonds is to quickly raise a large amount of capital, an amount that private banks aren't willing to, or perhaps, able to loan out, to complete projects. On the part of the government, these projects are happening every day, because we build new schools, roads, you name it, the possibilities, and the issued bonds, are endless.

So, why invest in a bond anyway, what's it going to do for you? As is with any type of investment, there must be a possible pay off. As with normal loans, the lender does get paid interest on the amount given. So, when you have a bond with the government or a corporation, you will be paid interest on however much money you invested. The exact percent interest paid annually varies on the bonds agreement, but you will receive an interest payment on a predetermined frequency, and when the term is up, meaning it has reached its "maturity", you will receive the entirety of your loan back. That percent interest is called a "coupon" and is derived by utilizing both the purchase price of the bond, as well as the associated coupon rate. As an example, check out this fixed interest scenario:

Bond Purchase Value: $5,000
Coupon Rate: 2.5% paid annually over 10 years
Annual Coupon: $5,000 *.025 = $125
Profit: $125 * 10 = <u>$1,250</u>

In this example, you'll see how we utilize a fixed interest rate instead of a compounding interest rate. This is intentional, as bonds utilize fixed interest rates. As can be seen with in this example, interest types differ between stocks and bonds. Similarly, actually purchasing bonds happens a bit differently than it does when purchasing stocks. Whereas with a stock, you can look up the ticker name and purchase a share directly through your broker, bonds don't work that way. I'd liken bond investment to commodity investment, in that, there is a direct way to go about it, but it's not preferable, and there's the more passive way to go about, which is definitely more beneficial. The best way to proceed is by investing in a Mutual Fund or ETF that specializes in, or contains bonds! This is not to say that you can't purchase bonds through your broker, you certainly can, as "resold" bonds are up for grabs at most popular brokerages. However, because these bonds are being resold, they're not the best buy, as the purchase price will usually be quite a bit inflated. Rather, if you're SUPER interested in purchasing bonds as an individual investor, you can purchase fresh bonds, which are sold at wholesale prices, from the government or from brokerages. There is an issue of accessibility in this scenario, as purchasing bonds usually requires quite a bit of capital. All of this boils down to one sound piece of investment advice, in respect to bonds, for the newbie investor: look into a bond fund! Anyways, without knowing it, most people invest in popular ETF's and Mutual Funds that already contain a good amount of bonds, so it's likely that you're already heavily invested in these types of investments, and you just don't know it.

What are the upsides of investing in bonds? First and foremost, bonds are definitely a safer bet than stocks. We've talked about how stocks are volatile, and the value of a given stock can dip based on a variety of factors, making it a risky investment. Even worse, if a company goes bankrupt, you risk going down with them. With bonds, especially those issued by credible vendors like the U.S. Government, the default rate is incredibly low. People bank on the fact that, based on their investment in government issued bonds, they will receive a steady income, and for the most part, this is a belief that has been backed by investor trends within bond history.

Sort of acting complementary to that, there is a separate form of bonds called "zero coupon bonds", where the investment strategy is a bit different, but offers advantages, still. Essentially, the bond is sold to the investor at a discounted price, but the investor will eventually be able to sell it for a much higher price. So, though you do not receive any annual coupons, you will benefit from having purchased the bond at a deflated rate. This type of bond investment isn't the popular choice amongst retirees because they are primarily looking for a passive, monthly income in the form of coupons.

Another upside of bond investing is passive management. There are entire mutual funds and ETFs that are solely dedicated to bond investment. So, by contributing to funds like this, you can benefit both from professional management of your bonds, where managers will attempt to maximize your earnings and lower any possible tax penalties, as well as not having to manage any of these costly investments yourself. Additionally, as we've said, because bonds require quite a bit of capital to invest in, entering into bond investment via a mutual fund or ETF, which have generally low costs to get involved, they are the preferred and more accessible way of getting in on some bond action.

Lastly, when deciding whether to invest in straight bonds or bond funds, you should be aware of how they behave differently. Bonds will provide you with the same monthly, or annual payment, as it's a guaranteed agreement that you entered into at the time of purchase. Bond funds, however, act like normal funds in that they provide you with fluctuating monthly dividend payments. Additionally, another point of difference is risk. With normal bonds purchases, if you hold that bond through to maturity, you're not affected at all, because it is up to YOU to make the decision when to sell. With bond funds, the situation is similar to a normal fund, as these fund managers buy and sell bonds before maturity is reached, so incurring a capital gain or loss, along with the associated taxes, is a reality.

What are the downsides of investing in bonds? The biggest drawback of bond investment is that the rate of interest produced is way smaller than what you'd see in a stock, which makes hungry investors stay away from them when they can. Generally, people looking for aggressive growth aren't interested in bonds, whereas people who want a steady, but humble, earning are more attracted to them. In addition, bond funds tend to cost a bit more in management, meaning that this eats away even more at your overall profit. Another fact of bond fund investment that is a detractor is that while the premium to get involved is still much, much lower than it would be to just outright buy a bond, it still hovers around $1,000, which to the new investor might pose an issue of accessibility. Lastly, there is the possibility that if your Mutual Fund or ETF invests in the wrong bond, the corporation could go belly up, and regardless of that situation happening, if your bond fund sells before maturity, you might incur both capital losses, along with normal fund taxes. It is important to note, however, that if the company does go belly up, bond lenders are the first to get any meager payouts that the company is offering, and have precedence over other shareholders.

How do bonds affect portfolio allocations? Asset allocations are manually set allocations by an investor when they open up a 401(k), IRA, or other passively managed investment account. With brokerages, setting up an asset allocation manually is not possible, so you should monitor the entirety of your investments to ensure that the asset allocation is something you're comfortable with. To help their clients, most brokerages offer portals and dashboards that show you your asset allocations across your investments. Even still, many of the investment accounts you open that require an asset allocation often provide their recommendation based on your age and the type of growth you're looking for.

The general rule of thumb when deciding on asset allocation, which is spread across stocks, bonds, and cash, is to use the "100 rule". By subtracting your age from 100, you're given a figure to allocate your stocks towards. For example, let's take a 25-year-old who is investing by opening a Roth IRA account for the first time.

Investment amount for FY2019: $5,500
Stock Allocation: *[100]-[Age]* = 100-25 = 75%
Amount invested in stocks: $5,500 * .75 = $4,125
Bond Allocation: *100%-[Allocation]* = 100%-75% = 25%
Amount invested in bonds: $5,500 * .25 = $1,375

The idea behind this equation is that, as you start getting closer and closer to retirement, you start to allocate more of your more towards conservative investment opportunities, such as bonds. However, when you are younger, you have the room to make riskier moves, possibly benefiting greatly off them. Most financial analysts would generally advise that everyone still stick to 100 years as an upper limit, though now that people are living much longer than they have in years past, and as a result working a bit longer as well, some recommend that you change the "100" number to 110, or even 120. Changing that number provides you with a few more decades of aggressive growth opportunity, but of course this final determination is up to you.

Lastly, there is the discussion of cash, and how much of your asset allocation should be reserved for that. In my opinion, none. Set up a secondary savings account for yourself, and save cash there, but as far as your investments are concerned, utilize every dollar that you set aside for investment, on investment! Emergency funds and savings are really the only places you should store your cash.

Key Takeaways

✓ Whereas stocks entitle you to ownership of a company, bonds are just plain ole' loans that you're most likely giving out to the **Government**.

✓ Loans generally attract more *risk averse people* that are looking to set up a passive source of income, as repayment is pretty much guaranteed, and the rate of return is also predetermined.

✓ Bonds AREN'T for people that are looking to do more with their money. It's better to be risky when you're young, because the payout could be **monumentally** more than if you stick with bond investment alone.

✓ Like Commodities, stick to investment in bond-focused ETFs or Mutual Funds, going into bond investment as an individual is *complicated AND requires quite a bit of capital*.

✓ When figuring out portfolio allocation, stick to the **"100 rule"**, but be aware that with the rising retirement age, that number might be pushed out accordingly.

Chapter 14:
Investing Part VIII - Bull vs Bear Markets

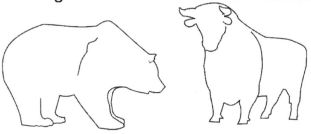

When reading articles about investment, most of the most common references you'll see will refer to terms like "Bull" or "Bear" markets. I remember when I was first starting to conduct research on the stock market, and used to watch YouTube videos from "financial pundits" who would use terms like these at least 80 times in the span of three seconds. My first impression of these guys was that they knew their stuff, because they were using these words that I had no contextual knowledge of. However, I slowly realized, after looking at different sources of information that you should not judge someone's financial acumen by the vocabulary that they utilize. So, while it's important to understand these terms, because it'll enable you to better understand a financial discussion should they be brought up, I would urge people to be wary of people who try to throw these, and other buzzwords, out in place substantive discussion. In fact, I would go so far as to say that people who make a point of talking in layman's terms are usually the finance gurus to follow, whereas the ones who use technical terms are just trying to make up for something they don't have - authentic knowledge.

Anyhow, these terms are essentially analogies utilized to describe broad characteristics of different market scenarios. One of the handiest tricks I've found to understand these analogies is to simply use the animal behaviors to distinguish how these animal behaviors relate to the stock market. Think of it this way, bulls reach for the sky with their horns, translating to the fact that the stock market is experiencing a situation where it's flourishing, and prices are being driven up, whereas bears swipe their paws down, meaning that the stock market is in a period of decline, and prices are being driven down. Bull and Bear markets work cyclically, and it is a good idea to understand the characteristics of both markets, as well as how they fall in a pattern, to anticipate how you need to modify your own portfolio to capitalize on the current environment.

Characteristics of a Bull Market. A "Bull" market comes into existence based on a simple law of supply and demand. When there is a greater demand, and a smaller supply, consumers are willing to pay more for products, meaning that this drives the market price up, and businesses, as well as the investors behind those businesses, profit. Generally, when bull markets exist, this means that it is a wonderful, flourishing time for the economy. This environment, in turn, creates a rippling sense of optimism for investors, who start to invest heavily in the market, which drives prices up even further, thereby creating a stronger and stronger bull environment. Bull markets can last for long stretches of time, even decades. Though there might be temporary phases of decline, the most important characteristic to view when trying to determine if the current market is experiencing a bull phase is whether or not a general upward trend is present.

When thinking of a Bull market, there's a strategy when it comes to investment, and the entire idea resides with the fact that prices are projected to go up. When a person enters into an investment under this premise, with the knowledge that the current environment characterizes a bull market, they're expecting that the price of the investment they purchased is going to increase, and they'll be able to sell it off for a higher price at a later date. So generally, during a bull market, people are incentivized to buy.

Characteristics of a Bear Market. Exactly opposite to the environment that a bull market creates, a bear market is generally a place of pessimism. Speaking in terms of supply and demand, bear markets arise when there is a great supply, but there isn't much of a demand, meaning that prices slowly fall lower and lower. This, in turn, effects the stock market when investors start selling off their investments at a much lower price than anticipated, further driving down prices. Once people become antsy and start selling off their stocks, they put that money into more risk-averse securities like bonds or even simple savings accounts. One important thing to also note is that, just like Bull markets, Bear markets will often have little blips that trick you into thinking that the economy is turning called "sucker rallies" so waiting it out a bit to see the overall trend before making your move is generally advised.

Unlike bull market strategies, bear market strategies are all about retaining your position, and at the same time, scooping up some good deals. Whereas every other person is probably making the panicked decision to sell off their investments and putting their money in a "safer" place because they see the losses being posted to their accounts, the smart investor firmly holds their position, rides off the wave, and waits for the Bull market to come back, which historically, we are pretty confident in saying, will happen. Another smart idea during this time is to actually buy. I know that sounds crazy, why would I buy when everyone else is selling off? Well, that's exactly the reason! Everyone is selling, prices are being driven lower and lower, and you can potentially nab a great deal. Buying at times of a bear market can prove to be a very beneficial move in the long run. The downsides of this strategy is the wait time involved. Some markets take VERY long to recover. An example is the Japanese market, which peaked in 1989, and has yet to recover, nearly 30 years later! So, while this might seem like a good move in the context of the American market, which generally takes less time to recover, it might not be the best move if you regularly utilize investment income or are involved in foreign markets who's trends you aren't familiar with.

At times like these, when money is hard to come by, the investor who decides to liquidate their assets and turn it into cash cannot be faulted. If you're right at the end of a bull market and after a couple months of decline, think that the economy is turning, and decide to liquidate your most vulnerable holdings, which would be the ones that are most inflated in terms of price, that's possibly a smart move. I'd definitely say that the investors in the Japanese markets that decided to sell at the end of 89' were happy with their judgement call. Of course, making the adequate analysis about which securities to sell off is of utmost importance, and selling EVERYTHING is not the way to go because when the market does recover, you won't be invested at all. Just like the Japanese market provides us with one extreme example, we can look towards our own American markets for an opposing example. There was a Bear period in the American markets from 2007-2008. People who purchased at the 2007 high saw nearly half of their invested become completely decimated, which was, no doubt a harrowing experience. However, the investors who kept their money invested throughout that Bear period saw, ten years later in 2017, a DOUBLING of their investment. The market was able to recover that much. For the investors that panic sold in 2008, they didn't end up reaping any of these benefits, instead, they just saw a loss. The general volatility of the market is just a tough topic in and of itself. Predicting how it will move is sometimes seen as an impossible science. Studying trends, reading reports from various sources, and holistically reviewing the health of your own portfolio are all important factors when making the difficult decisions to hold and sell during a Bear market.

Bull vs Bear Market best advice. One of the greatest tips an investor can utilize is knowing when the bull market is transitioning into a bear market, and vice versa. In personal experience, I started investing in the middle of a strong bull market, so one of the biggest things on my radar was, and still is, assessing the general health of the economy, watching trends, and hopefully catching the end of the bull market, so that I can adequately prepare for a bear market. I'm not Neo from the matrix, and so I'm just about as able as you to tell when the market will turn. My biggest advantage in this area is that I read. I read about market trends on a daily basis. The biggest pieces of news will hit the landing page of all the big financial websites, so "predicting" these turns is something I've left to a handful of diversified financial pundits that have benefited me in the past, and who's news I follow now.

In addition, one overlooked fact about investing is preparing yourself mentally for a downturn. Consider a young investor who starts out investing in the heyday of a bull market. Things are looking up, prices are being driven higher and higher, and profits are to be found nearly everywhere. When you develop a habit of expecting this profit, and then find that the market shifts to a bear market, of course the first gut reaction is to sell. However, the smartest investors are the ones that learn to grit their teeth through a downturn. It can be maddeningly troublesome to see your holdings dwindle, and honestly, if you can't envision yourself operating in daily life and bearing a downturn like that, investment is going to be difficult for you. Becoming an uneducated day trader and selling and buying where you see profit is also a horrible spiral to fall into, as you'll likely lose all your money. Think of the markets like a rollercoaster. Yes, you think you're losing your life when you take that first dip down, but eventually, you'll get back up, and in terms of the market, that up will get higher and higher throughout your life. Creating a mindset of consistency is important, choosing the correct investments is important, creating a diversified portfolio is important, and finally, holding your position is of utmost importance.

Key Takeaways

✓ Easy way to understand Bull vs. Bear markets: **Bulls** reach for the sky with their horns meaning the stock market is **flourishing**, whereas <u>Bears</u> swipe down with their paws, meaning the stock market is going <u>down</u> and generally not doing so hot.

✓ Bull markets exist because consumer sentiment is generally highly **optimistic**, meaning money is being thrown into the market. These periods can last entire decades!

✓ Bear markets, on the other hand, bring out a serious amount of **pessimism**, driving prices lower and lower. These periods can also last long periods, but they're also an opportunity to <u>buy stocks on the cheap</u>!

✓ Best advice? *Leave Bear + Bull market predictions to the expert.* You aren't a financial savant, so chill, keep up on the news and know when our economy is shifting, and prepare accordingly.

Chapter 15:
Investing Part IV - Robo-Advisors

In the growing age of tech, one of the biggest developments within the investment world has been the advent of robo-advisors. Many financial institutions, as well as standalone companies based entirely around this one service, are beginning to offer robo-advising. One interesting parallel that I noticed when I first started doing research on robo-investors is that they are very similar to the "millennial-friendly" online services that are offered these days. One big "disruptive" technique that manufacturers and service-providers are now utilizing is the personalization factor that a new age of consumers are coming to expect. For example, you have meal delivery kits, snack kits, clothing kits, and many similar services that allow the end user to personalize, to a certain degree, the end product that they receive. This personalization is usually achieved by the user taking a survey, thereby minutely varying the product they receive based upon user preference, which in turn allows the company to tout that they provide "tailored" solutions to users, whereas, at most, it's a pseudo-tailored product. Of course, this model has proven to be largely successful, as more preference-driven services are popping up daily.

Following suit, many financial institutions have adopted a similar model, where they allow the end user to advise a pre-created algorithm, which acts as a robo-advisor. Now, the general way to elicit preferences, which the algorithm will later utilize, is to either proceed with a survey, or present different "goals" to the user. The surveys will ask questions that will help the algorithm decide if the user is young or old, averse or not averse to risk, requires more investment capital stored as cash or not, and so on and so forth. Conversely, some robo-advisors allow users to set up separate accounts with distinct goals, like saving for a home, or saving for retirement. Based upon the goal, whether it's immediate or far-off, the algorithm will create a pre-set portfolio that differs based on "risk ratings" associated with these goals. Generally, platforms that are offered are pretty user-intuitive, catering to this subset of consumer who usually expect sleeker and more modern design, and even offer interesting investment strategies like investing all your change after you make a specific expense. The differentiated methods of investment that are offered are attractive to consumers because they have generally never been available through the more traditional financial brokerage institutions.

Taking a deep dive into the actual mechanics behind the operation, investment via robo-advisors platforms happens a bit differently than it would in traditional investing. As opposed to purchasing stocks, ETFs, or other securities for a certain share price, the way you invest in robo-advisors is sort of similar to how you would invest in a fund. You make an initial investment, which can usually be as low as $50, and continue to invest more in the platform as you have the cash, making it very user friendly as well as accessible to those users who don't have a lot of cash to start off. Now, as is with any type of investment, there are advantages, as well as disadvantages to evaluate.

Advantages of Robo-advisors. Well, right off the bat, one of the biggest draws of a robo-advisor is the, usually, cool interface they build for users. A robo-investing interface, in most cases, allows for personalized goal setting, as well as offers the end user graphical analysis of their investment in an intuitive display. Because marketing is such a big focus of drawing business for these robo-advisors, the types of services provided often most aligned to the tech savvy trends that modern consumers are drawn to. This is a very minute detail that will likely not affect the end result of how much money your investments are bringing in, but is one that attracts younger investors in particular because they associate sleek design with modern thinking. To give the robo-advisors some credit, looking at it through the perspective of a newbie investor, having these intuitive displays allows for an additional educational component, which is a significant advantage over traditional investing methods.

In addition to the intuitive interface, there is also the advantage of generally no human involvement in the management of your money. Yes, the algorithmic systems are managed and maintained by humans, but, the actual trades are conducted based on a system that doesn't have subjective feelings. So, whereas a fund manager might have a personal interest in conducting a specific trade, that entire component is removed when utilizing a robo-advisor. Now, I mention this because it's perceived as a general plus from investors. It's not to say that fund managers are out there conducting trades in the name of self-interest. There are fund managers that do that, but for the most part, this is a rare occurrence. Still, the fact that trades are conducted by utilizing an algorithm as opposed to human involvement is a factor to consider. Of course, there is the argument that a robo-advisor could be coded to make subjective trades based on the creator of the algorithm. But, when you think of it logically, the number of trades that are happening daily, for the number of accounts, requires a system that isn't coded for a company, ETF, or Mutual Fund, but rather, is coded to behave on a basis of Y/N answers, based upon a preset list of rules within a larger workflow. So, I feel confident in saying that robo-investors are more objective than fund managers based on the fact that one is a machine, whereas the other is a feeling human. However, realize that at the end of the day, these algorithms were created by the same fallible humans that you might fault for a bad investment mistake. It would be logically fallacious to say that an algorithm is infallible.

Another major draw of robo-advisors is the money management aspect. In most cases, these services are provided very low cost, often a nominal annual fee, whereas with typical trading platforms, you pay per trade. There are also options where you can task the robo-advisor with finding you the best in automated tax savings. Tax-loss harvesting, which is essentially a way to improve the tax return on your investments, is often a feature that you can turn "on" within a robo-advising platform for an additional cost.

Lastly, the hands-off aspect, on the part of the investor, is a factor that's beneficial for the newbie investor, and for investors in general. As far as selecting the portfolio, carrying out trades, and reinvesting dividends is concerned, the robo-advisor handles it all, without you having to make the judgement call on things that you might not be up-to-speed on. Passive investment, offered by robo-advisors, essentially requires minimal input from the investor, something that many people are drawn to.

Disadvantages of Robo-advisors.
Undoubtedly, one of the biggest advantages of robo-advisors also poses a serious disadvantage. Though some people find added security in the fact that the

robo-advisor is NOT a human, other investors are very much turned off by that. Many people prefer the human connection they have with a financial planner that they trust, especially when the bottom dollar is your money! People who aren't as technologically savvy might also be distrustful of algorithms in the sense that they don't want to get involved with something that they have little experience with. While I think this is mainly a generational gap issue in the true understanding of technology, I do believe that the outlook is warranted, because robo-advising is a rather nascent technology, having only existed since 2009. Since this technology has existed for such a small amount of time, nearly every trade is a test case for these companies. There is more to come in the way of improvements to the proprietary algorithms developed by these financial institutions, and in the meantime, the people utilizing these technologies, and the money they've invested, is financing a large-scale experiment of sorts.

Hand in hand with the discussion of this being a rather new advent of technology, is the idea that robo-advisors aren't totally prepared for a bear market. Ever since the creation of robo-advisors, the U.S. has been experiencing a bull market, meaning that all the experience these algorithms have is within a bull environment. Many people aren't totally convinced that these robo-advisor will be able to handle the real-time stressors of a transition from a bull to a bear market, and that money will be lost. An important thing to note from this perspective is that yes, money is lost in many different types of investments, especially during that critical shift between market types. Even if someone has the outlook that these robo-advisors will have difficulty making the transition, it's also important that they understand that, time and again, traditional fund managers have also had a great amount of difficulty handling this, and have lost money in the transition. So, to use this one factor to discredit robo-advisors isn't entirely a logical leap.

Additionally, I agree that the transition will be a great lesson to the maintainers of all the robo-advising algorithms as it will give them real life feedback. But, in advising investors who are wary of utilizing robo-investors for this case in particular, I'd say that the algorithms used are definitely put under a plethora of stress tests in a variety of different market conditions, and thereby attempt to simulate the knowledge that a fund manager would accumulate throughout their careers via experience. Of course, I too, am of the mind that human reactions still trump robo-advising in certain cases, as we're able to process information in a creative, and out-of-the-box way that isn't tied 100% to rules. However, overall, I believe that certain algorithms utilized by robo-advisors are strong contenders to traditional fund managers. Overall, robo-advisors will only benefit from a change in market condition, as they will continue to improve further upon their algorithms to make their platform stronger so that it can become a tried and tested investment tool in the next 20, 50, or 100 years.

So, should you really invest with a Robo-advisor? By now, you must know of my obsession with diversification, but with robo-advisors, I think the judgement call should be left with you. Many people chose to forgo involvement in a rather new technology and rely on tested mutual funds, index funds, and other related investments. There is a benefit in robo-advisors in that they are rather hands off, but we've discussed various methods of traditional passive investment that offer the same grade of passivity. If you want to diversify your portfolio even further, investing in a robo-advisor, learning with them over the years as the market makes the moves it's bound to make would be a cool and interesting education in a new investment technology. Some of the most preferred Robo-investors are offered by Betterment, Wealthfront, and WiseBanyan. Exploring the many algorithms that've been developed is also a useful research activity, as financial institutions like Betterment have created algorithms have been touted as "award winning". Overall, if you decide to go with one of these, check out the benefits, because some offer free services for College students, others offer free tax harvesting, and some even offer no minimum balances along with free management.

<u>Key Takeaways</u>

✓ Robo-investors are a **new advent** within the world of technology that allow for sleeker user interfaces and a pseudo-personalized investment experience. At the end of the day, the trades are being handled by an algorithm, as opposed to humans.

✓ There's a ton of positives behind robo-investing. You take possible corruption out of the equation as all trades are being considered as <u>Y/N events in a step-wise workflow managed by a computer.</u> In addition, many of these algorithms are award winning! They've proven their worth.

✓ With the positives...come the **negatives**! Many investors like the safety of knowing that a large team of humans are managing their funds, and are uneasy about automating something like investing. Fair play.

✓ Choosing to robo-invest is a personal decision. But if you're looking for personalized service, often very cheap, and are willing to invest in software that's still very much in the learning phase, then robo-investing might be for _you_!

Chapter 16:
Investment XIV: Dollar-Cost Averaging

At the College that I attended, there used to be this cool game room tucked away into a rather underutilized building on campus. It was called the Corner Pocket, and now I'm wondering if it still exists, and furthermore, wondering that if by mentioning it, perhaps I'm aging myself to all the people that still go to said school... Anyways, this place used to have a ton of different games, like Billiards, Table Tennis, Air Hockey, you name it. Each of these games was priced by the hour, so $5 for Billiards, or $3 for table tennis. Obviously, if you wanted to play for an extended period of time, paying per hour, per game, was both stupid and unfeasible. Instead, pooling money together was the move to make because you could reserve the entire corner pocket for specified amounts of time if you paid in bulk. So, a couple of friends and I used to keep a common pot, where we saved up $3 each week, and were able to reserve Corner Pocket for our personal use, for one evening each week, by paying an all-inclusive rate. This plan allowed us with access to all the games in the room, an exclusive space just for us, and it most importantly, it was cheap as hell. Yes! The nerds have won! Revenge of the Nerds! I've never seen that movie but hear it's good! We used the trickery of numbers to win against your own game, school, and now all the games belong to us! Muaha! Anyways...

The situation I'm trying to describe is one in which you gradually, and consistently save and invest. Proponents of an investment strategy called "Dollar-Cost Averaging", which follows this tenant, recommend it on the basis that there are huge benefits in consistency of investment. This principle is often true for most financial situations, including the very simple one of my friends and me attempting to save for a game night. Because every single week, without fail, my friends and I invested $3 to have Corner Pocket all to ourselves, we ended up, collectively, saving money. Had the twenty or so of us decided to play billiards or table tennis whenever we wanted, our money would've been wasted, while at the same time we wouldn't have access to exclusivity privileges. Now, this principle is also applicable to investing at times, and discussing the pros and cons behind this strategy is important.

Dollar-Cost Averaging is an investment strategy that is literally grounded in consistency in that it encourages the investor to make consistent investments on a predetermined schedule. When I was first getting into investment, I followed a methodology that comes second nature to most people. I would hoard a bunch of money, and then buy a huge, or at least what was huge for me, number of shares. Like most investors, I didn't have a clue as to the importance of developing an investment schedule, and whenever I had at least $1,000 saved up, I'd be so excited to just get an order in that I'd throw that entire sum in, all at once. Now, unlike hardline Dollar-Cost Averager's, I don't think there's anything detrimental about utilizing that, more simplistic methodology, but to truly understand both sides of the argument, it's important to look at a couple of use cases.

Advantages of Dollar-Cost Averaging. Now, when looking at putting large lump sum orders in, in the place of incrementally scheduled investments, proponents of Dollar-Cost Averaging often cite that the biggest issue at play is market predictability. It's true that it's literally impossible for you to know how a certain security is going to perform in the market, because that's all dependent on the million and one factors that affect our free markets. Of course, as we've discussed, there's things you can do to prepare for broad market shifts, like a bull market becoming bear, however, it'll be ALL over the news when a transition like that happens. However, the idea of you sitting behind your computer and clicking away at some matrix looking computer screen and predicting that one of your securities is going to dip 30% is, as I hope you realize, ridonkulous!

As a theoretical example, let's say I approached a purchase with the outlook of buying as many shares as I could, and not particularly caring about the cadence of my investments. I decide to outright purchase 10 shares of the Pear Company at the beginning of 2017. Those ten shares, priced at $300 per share, were purchased for a total amount of $3,000. Now, something catastrophic happened and the Pear Company is now in the throes of a massive PR Scandal, share price drops 30% down to $210 per share. Let's take a look at my projected loss:

> *Initial Price per Share (PPS):* $300
> *Purchase Price: [PPS] * [#]* = 10*300 = $3,000
> *Current PPS:* $210
> *Current Investment Value:* $2,100
> *Loss:* $900
> *Percent Loss:* 30%

Now, had I followed the tenets of Dollar-Cost Averaging, I could've saved out BIG with this investment. Let's say that from January 2017 to December 2017, I purchased 1 share of the Pear Company each month. Because the market is constantly fluctuating, each month I would've purchased a share for a different share price, and that the average of those (10) transactions was $257 per share. Let's take a look at our overall loss:

Average Price per Share (PPS): $267
Purchase Price: [PPS] * [#] = 10 * $300 = $2,570
Current PPS: $210
Current Investment Value: $2,100
Loss: $470
Percent Loss: 15.67%

As you can see, you changed absolutely nothing about the number of shares you ultimately purchased. But, by changing the cadence of your purchases, you were able to minimize your loss by nearly 15%. Of course, the idea is that after the PR Scandal, the Pear Company will recuperate itself, and you'll come out even stronger than had you made a bulk purchase.

Additionally, one of the reasons that this investment strategy resonates with people so much is because of the focus on the journey, as opposed to obsessively thinking about how much your purchase is going to make you. By implementing Dollar-Cost Averaging into your investment life, you set out with a goal to invest a preset amount of money, let's say $100, in a mutual fund you like, regardless of share price. You're making a commitment to a long-term investment, and are concurrently developing a mindset that won't quiver in the wake of market fluctuations. It is exactly these types of people, the ones who make consistent investments, and then hold onto them, that end up benefiting greatly over the course of multiple decades.

Now, a common factor that people bring up against Dollar-Cost Average, is trade fees. Yes, there are nominal trade fees associated with the purchase of a variety of different securities, as we've discussed. When you put an order through, it's normally around $5 per trade. People who oppose this strategy stress that submitting multiple trades causes investors to lose money because of the higher trade fees associated with this process. However, when you conduct a five-second cost-benefit analysis, you can easily see that the benefits of utilizing Dollar-Cost Averaging, if it works as intended, are far greater than any tiny trade fees you'll have to pay. The reasoning behind that lies with the fact that this is a long-term strategy. Over the course of many years, Dollar-Cost Averaging will help you stave off a significant amount of risk, thereby saving you much more than had you paid up front to buy a large amount of shares.

Disadvantages of Dollar-Cost Averaging. Now that we've viewed everything under rose-tinted, theoretical glasses, let's talk about reality. Vanguard conducted a study and found that in 66.67% of cases, people who invested lump sums ended up doing much better than people who'd utilized Dollar-Cost Averaging strategies. Now, there's a couple of reasons for that. The first reason is simply, exposure. If I have $5,000 and I invest it all immediately, that's going to translate to an immediate exposure to the market, for my investment. Whereas, if I stretch that $5,000 over the course of two years of investment, the latter parts of my investment are going to be very nascent, and for this reason, they aren't going to perform as well as an equal amount invested in a lump sum. So, while I'm not saying you'll lose money if you use Dollar-Cost Averaging, I am saying that, in most cases, you will end up making less, and that's just based on empirical evidence.

Now, the second reason is, that generally, the market is experiencing a period of growth, more than it experiences a period of decline. Because of this reason, the entire purpose of Dollar-Cost Averaging comes under fire, because the reason people utilize it is to minimize possible risk. In reality, when you view it from the scope of our own economy, you're mostly just minimizing exposure to growth, which is obviously a factor that plays against you.

Overall, do I think that you should utilize this investment methodology? I would recommend to you, what I recommended to myself, which was experimentation. If, within the course of a year, you follow a traditional path, ergo making a lump sum investment, then consider at the same time utilizing Dollar-Cost Averaging with another security, so you can better see which way works for you. I'm not saying that you should compare the rate of return, because these will be two very different securities. What I am saying is, figure out which mode of investment makes you feel more comfortable, and allows you to reach your investment goals for that year. Some people prefer to dump all their money in at once, and let it sit. Whereas others prefer to incorporate investment into their monthly budget. Lastly, one point to note is that if you truly know that you're a risk-averse person, and that potential risk in investment inordinately bothers you, implementing Dollar-Cost Averaging would go a long way towards relieving some of your stress, while still providing you with a solid rate of return.

<u>Key Takeaways</u>

✓ Dollar-cost averaging, in its essence, is an investment strategy used to invest on a <u>consistent schedule</u>, regardless of market performance. An example would be investing $100 into Apple stock every month.

✓ Proponents of dollar-cost averaging tout that the biggest pro of this method is that it **helps stave off risk**, because it averages share prices out between highs and lows, thereby providing additional padding against any major market dips.

✓ But, does it really work? There have been studies conducted by companies like *Vanguard* that show, in a prevailing sense, that investing money through Dollar-Cost Averaging usually results in lower gains.

✓ So? What's the play here? All in all, developing an investment methodology is important. Whether it be through stringent following of an invest plan based around dollar-cost averaging OR developing a game plan to invest 3x/year, whatever it be, don't leave your investment to guesswork, **<u>be intentional and be organized</u>**!

Chapter 17:
Investing Part X - Contrarian Investing

When I first starting out investing, I'll admit, I was often swayed by sirens to my left, and to my right. This was further compounded by the fact that as you and your peers grow, you all start getting into similar ventures, such as investment, and as a result there is ton of "advice" that goes around. In my personal experience, I received advice about how certain shares of an Irish gold company were going to EXPLODE in 2016! Similarly, I spent entire months hearing about how everyone and their mom was getting into cryptocurrency, and how, in 2018, that crypto was going to transform them into millionaires. Of course, none of those things happened. When starting out, it's definitely a difficult task to selectively, and intelligently, accept advice. One thing that's really helped me in this endeavor, is cultivating the appropriate mindset in relation to investment. To capture the type of ideology that I've tried to cultivate within myself, I'd like to share a quote from Warren Buffet, "Be fearful when others are greedy, and be greedy when others are fearful."

Like most people, I respond to FOMO with a sense of anxiety and panic. "FOMO" is an acronym for "Fear of Missing Out". Essentially, it's the feeling that if you don't participate in some prevailing group activity, you're going to be the one that's left behind. If I'm being honest, FOMO led me to majoring in science in College, as that was all my friends were doing. FOMO led me to booking vacations that I didn't particularly have much fun on, and FOMO has led me to at least 20+ brunches that I never wanted to go to! Essentially, FOMO can led to a serious leeching of cash, but when applied to investment, the financial fallout can be quite a bit more pronounced.

To understand out FOMO plays out in the investing world, a very good case to study is the Dotcom Bubble. In the late 90's, there were a ton of internet companies that came about, as a result of the rapid sophistication of web capabilities during that time. People started to flood these markets, investing in nearly every venture, even if it was absolutely ridiculous and had no merit. It was commonplace for the value of a new internet company's stock to more than double on its very first day of trading. Everyone in the market would characterize the situation as bullish, and people were throwing money in the collective pot to see a quick buck, as opposed to intelligent investing in a company that they believed in long-term. In fact, I'd feel safe saying that there was a significant amount of people at that time that didn't even have an idea of the type of product or service that the company they'd just invest $10,000 in, even provided. Things were THAT crazy! Well, as we all know, that bubble burst. After a few huge sell orders were put in by large corporations, the average Joe was alerted and people began the horrible tide of panic sells. Within a couple of months, companies who'd had market capitalizations in the hundreds of millions were folding. Over half of the internet companies founded during this time declared bankruptcy, closed their doors, and as a result posted extreme losses for investors. All of this, because of a little FOMO.

A piece of advice that would've been helpful for the investors of that time is relayed by one of the most prevailing idioms of our time, "Go against the tide". There is an importance imposed upon us within society to be an individual, and to think independently. But these things are difficult to accomplish, and it's far easier to just follow the crowd and hope for a reward that everyone else if banking on. However, at the end of the day, investments are very similar to your life, at large. Just like the individual choices you make affect your overall standing in life, your investment decisions will directly affect your financial wellbeing, so you literally can't afford to be lazy and just follow the crowd, it's imperative that you do your own research.

One of the safeguards that I've found that works best for me in determining if to make an investment move when there is a ton of hype in the market, is optimistic skepticism. It's in my nature, as it is with most of us, to want to be swayed by public opinion. Of course, I want to believe my cousin when he tells me that I'll never have to work again if I invest in this type of technology. However, analyzing the source of the information, in conjunction with the viability of the investment is of utmost importance, trusting people at their word, particularly when it affects your investment decisions, is a surefire way to lose money. You must put a premium on fighting the knee jerk response to "buy, buy, buy" when someone urges you, and instead take your time to develop your case, and make an informed decision.

The ideals that I've just described are encapsulated within an investment strategy. Contrarian Investing is a type of investment strategy that encourages the investor to go against the tide. When everyone else is panic selling, you hold on, and when everyone else is too scared to buy in the throes of a bear market, you buy. Though your decision-making workflow shouldn't be as simplistic as a quick scan of what the general populace is doing in respect to a security, taking that factor into consideration, and prioritizing it quite highly, should be a personal prerogative. Overall, tried and true methods of investing, where you both understand what you're investing in and believe in a future rate of return, are the ones that an investor should live by. Furthermore, padding that with a quick scan of general market trends, and analyzing whether hype, FOMO, and therefore illogical behaviors play a part in these movements, is a smart habit to form. Being swayed by public opinion, and letting media reports make your investment decisions for you is a very naive way to view investing, and will inevitably lead to the development of bad habits, like panic selling, as well as generally poor investment choices.

Now, utilizing personal research and contrarian methodologies at the same time can be highly beneficial to the investor. During the time of a bear market, researching which securities have a solid future, but are being undersold at the time, can result with a huge payday, assuming the correct decisions are made. For example, shortly after the dotcom bubble burst, Amazon was priced at $10 a share, and today, it's valued at $1,400 per share. People who did the appropriate research were able to scoop this up for a bargain, and after holding onto it for a while, benefited enormously.

Though we might not all be aware of it, FOMO continues to play a huge part of our investment lives, and there's at least one prevailing example every decade. Modern day examples of the dotcom bubble, and a way to put contrarian investing strategies to work, is within the realm of cryptocurrency. In late 2017, there was an enormous sense of hype surrounding cryptocurrencies and blockchain in general. Cryptocurrency is essentially digital currency that is sold in many varieties in the form of a coin. Some popular coins are Bitcoin, Litecoin, Ethereum, and Ripple. There came a time when certain coins that had no technology behind them, and were just being marketed as digital currency, had market capitalizations driven up to the billions because of uneducated investors throwing their money this way and that. The general hype that surrounded this technology was a hint for contrarian investors that they should abstain from investing, or if they chose to do so, they shouldn't do it in the quantities and methods that most other investors were utilizing. Everyone from middle schoolers to bus drivers were recommending that people should get into cryptocurrency. Nearly every day, there were reports out in the media about "Bitcoin Millionaires" who made that money based on a small $500 investment into the technology. Market capitalizations of some 1,200 different coins was driven up enormously. Everyone was buying in.

But, as a contrarian investor would be quick to point out, the sentiment wasn't consistent with that of sound investment. People were not investing because they understood the technology. I think it'd be safe to say that most people investing in cryptocurrency during this time had no idea what the technology behind it, blockchain, was, or be able to explain why this technology had a future. Rather, the big draw to investing in crypto, at the time, was to make a quick buck, which is a very similar situation as the one during the dotcom bubble. People were hoping to cash in and cash out within a couple of months, and during that time grow their money 10-fold.

Ultimately, because of rapid investment, and then blips of sell-offs, panic ensued, and the price was dragged down quite a bit, causing an all-out crash. Now, in the aftermath of this crash, people that believe in the future of blockchain, and associated cryptocurrencies, can utilize their contrarian investment strategies to research which coins are being sold at a discount, and based on current utilization, might peak in the coming 5, 10, or 15 years. Even more intelligently, investors could look for possible mutual funds or ETFs that specialize in cryptocurrencies, which allows for another layer of security and professional management. Overall, regardless of whether you bought or not, the underlying importance is that if you bought, you did it for logical reasons, and not as a reactive response to market hype. Maintaining your position, watching others, and ultimately the trends they create, and acting only after you have an educated understanding of the current market environment are all contrarian ideals that you should stick to.

Overall, even if you aren't a diehard contrarian, and don't want to make that the hallmark of your investment ideology, it's helpful to pick up a couple of tips from this proven methodology. Be optimistically skeptical - question everyone and everything when it comes to investment, because the more you become educated on something BEFORE you make a move, the greater the chance that it'll end up being beneficial. In that spirit, look at the stuff that no one seems to be paying attention to. This thought can be applied to crypto as well. If, for example, everyone is looked at Bitcoin and Litecoin, take a look at other coins that might already have been adopted by companies, are being utilized, but are being overlooked by most investors, perhaps investing in those coins is where the benefit will lie 20 years from now. And finally, don't get caught up in the zealous nature of the market. If you don't understand something, learn to live with the FOMO until you can make an informed decision, because we've all had FOMO led us to a brunch where we put down $40 for bad company, a horrible omelet, and a sunburn.

Key Takeaways

✓ If you take **ANYTHING** from this chapter, let it be the fact that FOMO is a bad reason to do *basically anything* in your life, and, investment.

✓ Contrarian Investment is a type of mindset towards investment that encourages people to go against the tide, if the masses are selling, think about buying, and if everyone from your uncle Gary to your weird coworker Janis is buying a security, maybe it's best to stay away from it.

✓ An incredible amount of **foresight** is required for Contrarian Investing. For example, panic selling is something that comes second nature to most of us, but having the resolve and foresight to hold onto a security is incredibly challenging, and is a skill that people should slowly build.

✓ Overall, it's not important that you become a diehard contrarian investor, BUT, starting to reflect on what everyone else is doing, and whether that's a valid move, i.e. slowly building a questioning nature towards investment, is an invaluable journey to start yourself on.

Chapter 18:
Investing Part XI - Real Estate

Having experienced the housing market crash in the late 2000's, most people are familiar with the concept of "flipping". It was pretty interesting to see the increase in business that HGTV, and similar home design channels, saw as a result of something that would've seemingly brought their viewership down. However, because housing prices hit a rock bottom and many properties were being sold for pennies on the dollar, that increased accessibility inspired an entrepreneurial set of people to take advantage of the situation and begin remodeling homes and selling them off for a profit. This in turn spurred the creation of hundreds of different shows that depicted anything from a set of twins flipping and selling homes, to ranchers in Texas dragging a rig from Alaska to Austin in order remodel mobile homes. Now, with flipping, you must understand that this is one, very specific way to invest in real estate. It is by no means the most popular, or the most profitable, but because of the 50+ shows on TV that detail this process, most people are very familiar with it. Instead, there are many more passive, as well as some active, ways to get involved with real estate investment and potentially create a second stream of income.

House Hacking. One of the prevailing ways that newbies become landlords, and start amassing many rental units, is by starting small. A scary fact is that once you're independent, a huge chunk of your salary will go towards shelter, something that most people take for granted when mooching off their parents for the first 20ish years of their life. If you're living in or near a major city, that chunk could possibly amount to HALF of your take-home pay each month, so increasingly, we're seeing trends where people resort to creative avenues to decrease that housing cost. House Hacking is a prime example of one of those "creative" avenues. The general idea behind House Hacking is that you purchase a large building, one which has multiple units within it, and by occupying one of those units, you can utilize a normal residential loan, and then rent out the rest. After crunching the numbers, you'll find that most house hacks are able to enable the homeowner with 100% free living because of the rental income provided by renting out other units within the building. The tenants that you keep will essentially be paying your mortgage for you, allowing you to live expense free. In addition, if you want to make active real estate investment your career one day, this is a great first step and sort of a trial-run in both maintaining a landlord-tenant relationship as well as carrying out the responsibilities associated with being a property manager.

It should be noted that most of the buildings purchased for this reason are absolute nightmares when you first get them, and that serious remodeling must be done to make them livable. Part of this is because people purchasing a house intended for house hacking, usually don't have a lot of capital to

135

start out with. The remodeling requires both cash, as well time and dedication, so this definitely does NOT qualify as a passive source of investment, as you will be getting your hands dirty throughout the duration of this arrangement. However, the potential payoffs are huge. One major piece of appreciation is any remodels you do to the building will cause its value to appreciate significantly, and of course, over time, as property values increase, you'll hopefully be able to sell this property off for a profit, meaning that you incurred no cost at all throughout the period you were involved in this investment. Most importantly, every month, when your tenants pay your mortgage, you're essentially building "free" equity, that's money in the bank!

Outside of the "traditional" house hacking methods like renting out a space in a duplex, triplex, or fourplex, there are also other avenues you might want to explore. If you live in the city, where parking costs are astronomically high, and don't have a car, you can create a passive source of income anywhere in the $50-$500 ballpark for you parking spot. Additionally, if you travel for work, or have a spare bedroom, based on your building's sublet policies, you can set up an Airbnb arrangement. I have friends that are able to pay off the entirety of their mortgage by renting out one of their bedrooms on Airbnb for one week a month! That extra monthly income can be applied to so many things, particularly, to savings and investments.

Purchasing Multiple Rental Properties. Now, one step beyond house hacking is becoming a full-blown rental property investor, by starting to manage multiple properties that all bring in passive sources of income. Would it sound crazy to you if I said that there are many people out there that own and manage 25+ rental properties? Well, it's the day-to-day for many rental property investors that look at their rental earnings as their main income. Based on the mortgage that you work out for the property, you could be looking at a $100-500 surplus each month, after you use the rent that you collect to pay the mortgage. If you spread that across multiple properties, you could be making $5-10K each month on passive income from rental properties.

When thinking about getting financing for these properties, it's important to note that utilizing the earnings from one rental property, and putting it into another is a good way of making an early investment to amass a greater number of properties. Technically, the more money you put down in the property, the better your mortgage will be, and the greater your monthly surplus. So, having adequate cash savings prior to expanding from one property to another would be advised, though many people choose to expand the number of properties they have in the quickest way possible, by taking out mortgages that might not be particularly good in terms of long-term value. A caveat to that, however, is that most people proceeding with this plan of action make it a point to form close relationships with small banks in their area. These banks both understand the work the investors are doing, trust their process, and most importantly, are willing to finance the multiple properties that they plan on purchasing.

But, exactly how complicated can this situation get? I would caution people who are looking seriously at this idea with the fact that this sort of lifestyle is best suited for a particular type of individual. When managing multiple properties, you'll be dealing with many tenants, all of whom have issues. In a given day, you might deal with people who break their leases, causing you to have a vacancy that you need to fill immediately, or you might deal with a break-in, or a dishwasher malfunction, the possibilities are really endless, unfortunately. I've seen friends of mine try to set this situation up while maintaining a full-time job, and all of them mostly crumpled under the pressure, because it's an extremely stressful position yourself in. If are you going to devote yourself to this lifestyle, I think it'd almost be imperative that you make this your sole focus. You can help alleviate this burden by hiring a property manager, but still, this is a huge commitment that shouldn't be looked at for someone that is in search of a truly passive investment.

Flipping Houses. Ok, time to put all the knowledge I've amassed from House Hunters and the Remodeling Twins to use! Even though I don't particularly want to, a discussion on flipping houses is warranted. My lack of desire to discuss this topic stems largely from the fact that I believe is a risky endeavor, and I don't know how much I'd personally recommend it. However, let's get to a discussion of how flipping operates. The general schema for flipping houses is purchasing a home for a low price, remodeling it by utilizing a realistic budget, and then selling it for a profit. From start to finish, there are a ton of moving pieces involved in flipping homes, and a lot of trial and error is involved in attaining the expertise that's required to be a successful flipper, so it's definitely not for the faint of heart.

First and foremost, these people have access to (2) very important things that most people probably don't: capital and housing market knowledge. To make a good deal off a flip, you must know how to get a deal. Studying housing prices in the area, and knowing when a house is priced drastically below what it could potentially be worth, if flipped, is of utmost importance. Because many of these sales are often short sales, involving foreclosures, it becomes even more important to be able to quickly assess a home, make the correct decision, and then have the capital on hand to purchase said home. Because there isn't a ton of time to arrange for mortgage, many of these homes are bought on cash.

Post-purchase, there's a new can of worms to deal with: remodels and contractors. If you get stuck with a bad contractor, who either charges too much, takes too long, or does crap work, your entire flip could be derailed, and you could lose a ton of money. Having a trusted contractor that gives you an honest rate, honest work, and an honest timeline is going to save you SO much grief. So, doing the due diligence required to find that individual is very important. In addition, if you're able to complete work that you know how to do yourself, along with a contractor to do the heavy lifting, you can save on some of the labor costs for simpler activities.

Finally, after all that work, that spans months, potentially even a year (though not longer than that, or you're losing out by paying the rent every month for a property that is not generating any income), you must sell the place. The faster you sell it, the less negotiations that occur with the buyer. So, again, knowing how to price the home well, and sell it quickly is super important. Potentially, a good flipper can make a profit of $50K in a span of four months on one flip. Multiply that across multiple flips occurring at the same time, as you build capital from sales, and you could build a flipping empire. But, as you can tell, this process is nerve wracking, stressful, and dependent on many factors that could go awry.

Do people lose money flipping? YES! In 2016, it was reported by RealityTrac that 40% of flips either sold at break-even or below cost. After all that effort and time, where you were likely not generating any other income, you actually LOST money. It's very common for a novice flipper to pay too much upfront, pay too much during the remodel, have a bad contractor that extends the timeline or myriad other issues that could lead to no profit, or even a loss. Making it in this business requires time, effort, and trial and error. There will be losses, but as you learn, you can potentially become a stronger flipper. Of course, more people tend to like the idea of buying and holding property, and renting it out, as opposed to aggressively flipping and selling multiple times in a year.

Invest in REITs. REITs are real estate investment trusts. These trusts allow an investor to invest in real estate, without ever having the added responsibility of maintaining a physical space. The trusts that investors put their money in own a bunch of buildings ranging from offices, to homes, to industrial plants. Now REITs can be purchased similarly to a regular share. Publicly traded REITs can be purchased on brokerage portals, though there are private varieties that are not kept on the stock exchange. As a result, public REITs offer some of the same benefits that other shares offer. They have professional management, meaning that this allows for a passive way of investment for lenders. In addition, REITs offer liquidity, meaning they can be bought and sold as per the investor's discretion. Some of the added benefits that draw in older consumers is the fact that REITs pay huge dividends. This isn't a con for younger investors though, they can simply choose to fold that divided back in and grow their investments even more.

Historically, REITs are one of the best performing asset classes, and investing in them is something that is recommended by most people in finance, as it helps diversify your portfolio, and one day, will provide you with a steady source of income via dividends. When constructing your portfolio, you should take time to include REITs that have historically performed well to attain a good level of diversification.

Real Estate, is it worth it? Overall, yeah, I would say real estate investment is a "worth it" activity. However, depending on the level of involvement you want with your investment, there's definitely a specific way to go about it. For the traditional investor, who maintains a steady source of income, and is looking at investments as a good way to create wealth and retirement income, a passive way of investing, namely REITs, would be the prescribed method. Whereas if you're an investor who is looking to make real estate income your primary income, it would be prudent to start considering house hacking, and potentially move towards either investing in additional rental properties, flipping homes or both. Of course, with either course of action, passive or active investment, it's important that the investor do a good amount of research before diving in, as making an uneducated choice is a surefire way to lose cash.

Key Takeaways

✓ If you're interested in entering real-estate investment, one of the best ways to get involved is by **house-hacking**, where you purchase a larger building (think fourplex), renovate it on the cheap, and rent out units in order to cover the mortgage, and make some extra *ching chang*.

✓ Another popular form of real estate investment is becoming a landlord for a large number of properties. If you want real estate investment to be your **MAIN** job, start buying properties, renting them out, and using the profits to purchase more properties. People who follow this method slowly build up passive streams of income that value at $400/property, and they own somewhere in the ballpark of 20-25 properties! TBH this is a <u>pretty stressful</u> empire to build so proceed cautiously.

✓ House flipping is something that most of us are familiar with BUT it is <u>not something I'd 100% recommend</u>. Especially in current times, with a recovering housing market, it can become incredibly stressful for a newbie flipper to properly source material and hire reliable labor, which isn't even related to the compounding factor of actually selling the home. All in all, making a profit using this method is become harder and harder.

✓ Lastly, REITs, real estate investment trusts, are one of the best performing classes of investment, pay huge dividends, offer high liquidity, and are a much more passive form of investment that <u>still allows access to those interested in real-estate investment</u>.

Chapter 19:
Investing Part XII: Tax Penalties

We've spoken about taxation loosely throughout this book, wherever it was relevant. For example, we've discussed taxation and penalties in bits and pieces, ranging from how they are related to topics ranging from withdrawing early from pre-tax retirement funds to the tax harvesting options that robo-advisors offer. However, there are overarching annual taxes that all investors should be aware of, and furthermore tailor their portfolios and holding strategies to avoid.

Capital Gains Tax/Capital Losses. First to bat is the lovely Capital Gains tax. This taxation is a great way for the Government to "encourage" investors to hold onto their investments for longer periods. In a sense, the Capital Gains Tax discourages aggressive trading techniques like day trading by imposing a rather large taxation on activities as such. However, normal activities that you might try to conduct on your account might also fall under this category.

As an example, let's say you purchase 10 shares of Company X for $200 a share, totaling $2,000 worth of investment. If at any point and time, from day 0 to day 365, you choose to sell that share for a profit, the gain that you made as a result of that investment will be taxed at your normal income tax rate, which is usually pretty high, hovering around 30% for most middle-class people, and even higher for people who earn more. However, if you decide to hold onto that investment for 1 year and 1 day, or longer, you'll be taxed lower, which for most people, falls to around 15% (but can be higher if you are a very high earner). Let's simulate this example to see the potential earnings LOST as a result of selling early:

Sold Prematurely
Initial Share Price: $200
Initial Investment: $2,000 (for 10 shares)
Final Share Price: $250
Gross Earning: [F]-[I] = $2,500-$2,000 = $500
Net Earnings: $500 - ($500*.30) = **$350**

Sold 1+ Years later
Initial Share Price: $200
Initial Investment: $2,000 (for 10 shares)
Final Share Price: $250
Gross Earning: [F]-[I] = $2,500-$2,000 = $500
Net Earnings: $500 - ($500*.15) = **$425**

Take it from me, this is a super *simple* example, and usually earnings are not as clear cut as this, but it gives you a roundabout answer of the fact that you're missing out on cash if you sell early. In this example alone, this meant a 30% reduction in overall earnings! If you extrapolate this over an investment that's worth $20,000+, you can see how selling your investments early is essentially throwing cash out of your pocket.

Now, this is not to say that selling prematurely is always a bad decision. There are certainly situations in which the smartest move is to sell off your holdings, cash out, and reinvest in perhaps a more stable investment option. Situations like this might arise if you suspect a company that you're invested in is about to south, meaning that a possible recuperation down the road is very unlikely. Additionally, if a price hits an all-time high, and due to an analysis of the market environment, you sense that this price might not continue to increase, it would advantageous to sell at this point, and perhaps buy back-in at a lower point. These are just some, very specific, scenarios, and shouldn't be understood as hard and fast rules, because, as always, an in-depth analysis should be conducted prior to panic buying or selling. The overall point I'm trying to make is that if you're in a stable investment relationship, it might be worth it to wait until a year's up to sell the holding. In my mind, of course I would encourage even longer term holding of securities, because that's where you'll see your real wealth growth as a result of continued compounding interest.

One last thing point to bring up about Capital Gains prior to moving onto a discussion of Capital Losses, is the concept of Funds. When you're involved in a Mutual Fund, Index Fund, or any type of Fund really, these Fund Managers might sell off investments prematurely. This is always a point of reason that people advise not getting involved with Mutual Funds. Proponents of this type of thinking advise people to get involved with ETFs, where you just don't create as many taxable situations as you would when involved with a traditional fund. It's true, and you should be aware of the fact that, when a Fund Manager decides to sell off these holdings prematurely, which is commonplace with many Mutual Funds, that tax burden falls to your shoulders. However, by and large, Mutual Funds do work extremely hard at avoiding shoving short term capital gains onto their lenders, so doing a good bit of research into the particular mutual fund to see trends in relation to this issue, prior to investing, would be a good bet tax-wise.

Now, one way the Government attempts to console an investor whose portfolio performed poorly that year, is by helping him or her out with the tax bill. Capital Losses, much like Capital Gains, reflect the investment activity you've had over the prior year. Acting complementary to Capital Gains, Capital Losses describe any losses you've incurred from the sale of a long-term or short-term investment holding. However, if you have an active investment, that you haven't sold, but has lost value over the past year, it's essentially meaningless in tax world, because you can't report unrealized losses, rather, only realized losses are reportable.

Essentially, when you fill out your tax return for that year, you categorize your Capital Gains and Capital Losses into short-term and long-term holdings. The net of that equation (Capital Gains - Capital Losses), is ultimately the Net Capital Gains that you are taxed on. So, if you do have a bad year, and incurred a good amount of loss, you can use that number to ask Uncle Sam for a bone, and avoid some extra taxation for that year.

Dividend Taxation. Like Capital Gains, any dividends that you receive in each year are also viewed as taxable income by the Government, which is definitely a bummer, but it's a reality you should embrace when building a portfolio that includes high dividend paying stocks. Dividend taxation, because it's viewed as another source of income, is also taxed in a corresponding scale. Generally, if you're in the bottom two tax brackets, you don't have to worry about dividend payments. However, anything above that brings anywhere from a 15% to a 20% taxation on your dividend payouts.

One cool trick to avoid Dividend tax, and continue growing your investment is investing in your 401(k), IRA, or other retirement investment account. Any dividends incurred within these accounts cannot be touched for taxation purposes, so they're just reinvested and you get to reap the benefits from a growing portfolio.

Real Estate Taxation. So, before getting started, one should be cognizant of the fact that taxation on real estate is a topic that can get very complicated if you start investing in multiple rental properties, so if that's a path you're going down, educate yourself so that you don't have taxation issues down the road. However, for the ordinary investor, one should know a couple of things. First off, real estate is taxed similarly to other investments, in that the profit made from the sale of a property is viewed as income, and that short- and long- term gains are applied to this concept. One awesome fact about selling homes, however, is that the sale of a personal home, should you meet certain criteria like age of home ownership and amount of years resided within said home, is that it's tax-free up to about $250,000 worth of profit, which is awesome!

Lastly, one point to make on real estate investments is the concept of depreciation.

Essentially, the depreciation concept allows an investor to claim a deduction based on the cost of that home. This number is split up amongst 28 some years, during which time, you'll be able to deduct a fraction of the overall depreciation annually. If you're someone that owns a large amount of rental properties, even though you might not be experiencing any depreciation in the physical estate, you'll be able to claim that deduction, and see a huge lowering of your overall tax bill. Definitely a concept to explore more in detail for investors who plan on owning multiple, physical properties that they maintain.

Overall, taxation is something that, large and in part, you can't really avoid. Like Taxation happens on your income, it happens on any investments that you make. The best thing that you can do is investigate how to construct your portfolio to play as intelligently as possible within the rules. Though I don't believe that taxation, alone, should be a defining reason for you to choose to invest in a certain avenue of investment, or not, it's definitely one of many factors that you should take into serious consideration when making that educated choice.

<u>Key Takeaways</u>

✓ The lovely **Capital Gains Tax** is an annual tax imposed by the United States Government on people who prematurely (meaning the security is held less than a year) sell off their holdings. It's basically an incentive to hold onto a security for longer than a year.

✓ Remember! Selling securities is not always 100% if your hands. Yes, if you own individual shares, buying & selling is all on you. BUT if you've invested in a mutual fund, they can sell stuff off prematurely, not really make any money off it, and then pass that taxable amount onto you, because, at the end of the day, it's YOU that owns it. **Be aware!**

✓ With the bad, comes the good. If your portfolio performs poorly in a given year, the Government <u>DOES throw you a bone</u>, in the form of Capital Loss declaration, where you can basically list out all your losses, which will that be factored in and lower the amount of tax you owe for that year up to a certain limit.

✓ Remember how much we love dividends? Well, at the end of the day, they're seen as INCOME, and as a result, taxed. There are ways to avoid this, by rolling this income straight into a <u>pre-tax retirement account</u> (like a 401(k)).

✓ Lastly, real-estate does get taxed. But, when you sell a personal home, barring certain criteria, $250,000 worth of profit is **100% tax-free!**

Chapter 20:
Common Financial Goals

Though, up until now, there has been a concerted effort to impress upon you the importance of establishing sound savings and investment techniques, at the end of the day, this is essentially just a means to an end. The reason people go through this cycle of educating themselves on personal finance and becoming smarter on the subject, is to accomplish personal goals that they've set for themselves. Full disclaimer, I am aware that financial goals vary greatly from person to person. I remember being particularly inspired by a friend of mine in College who worked tirelessly, for four years, at our campus cafeteria to save $20,000. Throughout that time, he was very vocal about his dream to travel the Country after he graduated. And, even though he had a degree in Finance, and was smart enough to land a job essentially anywhere, he instead decided to convert an old camper and travel to, and hike in all the National Parks in the United States. Of course, to "camp" in nature is not a goal that I, personally, would ever aspire towards, I can of course appreciate the vision, and related consistency that was required to achieve something like that.

Though this is a very unique example, the underlying journey is one that's very relatable. One thing that both he, and any ordinary person who has a pointed goal, have in common is resolve. As you grow older, you start to realize that while having an active imagination is actually a great advantage, in that it allows someone to creatively envision personal goals for themselves, it's nothing without an actionable plan. If my friend had talked for all those years about doing what he wanted, but hadn't devised an actual way of financing that plan, there's no way he would've had the life changing experience. And so, in approaching any goal in life, be it attending law school and earning your J.D., or simply owning a car that you always dreamt about owning as a child, you must write down, and meticulously track, how you plan on getting there. Most goals also have a financial "sub-goal" to them, so tracking towards attainment of that financial sub-goal is also of utmost importance.

Throughout most of this book, the discussion on investment has been focused around retirement savings. Of course, retirement savings should hold key importance in your life. With the rising trend of Americans having saved close to nothing at the time of retirement, this is a real problem that affects large swaths of society, and is one that you want to actively work to avoid. However, aside from retirement, there are more immediate goals in the life of a young 20-something that hold precedence. In this chapter, I'm going to discuss some common financial goals that someone in their early 20's would have, and detail certain issues to consider when devising a game plan to accomplish them.

Owning your first car. One of the first issues I faced straight out of College was the car problem. Throughout school, when I was living on campus, I, like most College bums, didn't have a need for a car. If I needed to get off campus, I'd politely asked one of my more blessed friends who actually had a car, and when I needed to get home, I'd call my dad. Things change when you graduate, friends. All of a sudden, I lived 40 miles away from my job. I tried the bus life, it wasn't for me. Three changes, a two-hour commute ONE WAY, and a weird man sitting next to you every day when there are literally 80 open seats will do horrible things to your personal health. I even tried to get my parents to pick and drop me off from my teaching job. Yes, the science teacher was rolling up in the kiss n' ride lane, my students certifiably got a huge kick out of that one. Ultimately, I decided that I had to bite the bullet and get a car.

When thinking of getting a car, the first big question to ask is whether you'll own or lease. For most people, this is a no-brainer. "Why would I essentially pay to rent a car, when I could just pay a similar monthly fee and own it?" Though that seems to be the knee jerk reaction, the answer to this question is based largely on your planned life situation. Being very intentional about your long-term goals, and relating that back to a vehicle purchase has the potential to save you a massive amount of money. Of course, if you're planning on owning a particular vehicle long-term, leasing would end up being costlier to you. However, some solid reasons to lease, because they're not usually that apparent, would be if you're planning on going back to school after a couple of years in the workforce. In situations like this, where you're looking for flexibility, as opposed to signing off on a 20-year agreement, a lease can come in very handy. There's no rhyme or reason as to why a person who plans on returning to school would purchase a vehicle, and then be saddled with parking, taxes, and gas on a mode of transportation that they don't need. In this, you'll see the importance of having intentionality and forward thinking in respect to big financial decisions, like buying a car. If you mindlessly make the decision to buy right out of school, and you don't forecast far enough out in your life, you're going to end up leeching money left and right.

Now, there is the third option, which is buying used. Of course, you can choose to buy a used car, and again, that's a personal decision. The obvious detractor of purchasing a used car is that, even with these guarantees of 100% car history, you never really know. And, once that deal is done, and six months in your car gives out on you, you're shit out of luck! Whereas when I was in High School, and College, I purchased used cars, because they were so cheap, I've switched my mentality since leaving school. Personally, I believe it'd be far more advantageous to pay a premium price for a quality product, as opposed to the risk of having to cycle through a multitude of used cars because of repeated issues, but, to each their own!

Now, for me, the decision between leasing and buying was a difficult one to make, but I ended up going with leasing. It offered me flexibility because it didn't tie me down to a long-term auto loan agreement. Additionally, by taking advantage of leasing offers for recently graduated individuals, which usually means a bit of a discount, in addition to a Holiday special over Veteran's Day, I was able to work out a deal I was comfortable with. An added bonus of leasing is that the monthly costs associated are usually very reasonable, making it budget friendly to someone who is paying off debt or school loans, and in addition, down the road if you do totally fall in love with your vehicle, you have the option of buying it off the dealer once your lease is over.

Owning your first home. Another big step in the life of a young 20-something is buying their first home. With homeowner trends changing as of late, however, it is true that most homeowners are well beyond their early to late 20's when they make their first home purchase. Regardless, there is information you should know prior to making that first plunge. Of course, straight out of school, you'll likely be living with your parents, or sharing an apartment with multiple people, and that is a smart move! When you look at it for what it is, renting a home is just you paying someone else's mortgage. So, if you can spread the burden amongst a couple of roommates, you're better off for it.

It's sage advice that as soon as you are financially able, you should look into owning a home. The longer you wait to own a home, the more you utilize your hard-earned cash to pay someone else's mortgage, thereby foregoing years' worth of equity that you couldn't built for yourself! One of the biggest issues young people face in terms of owning a home is accessibility. Because of the pretty intimidating amount of funds you need to buy an average place, most young people, who spend erratically in the first few years on the job, aren't able to position themselves in such a way as to achieve homeownership during their 20's. However, there are both programs, as well as person habits, that one can tap into in order to make that goal a reality.

Now in the context of first time homebuyers, there are government programs that make owning a home more accessible. First off, looking at the financial burden of both a monthly rental payment vs. a monthly mortgage, you'll see that the two don't have much of an appreciable change. Of course, if you're transitioning from a rental agreement in which you're sharing the burden amongst a bunch of people, making that transition to owning a mortgage will be an adjustment. However, for the most part, mortgage payments tend to be a bit lower than a traditional rental agreement. If you think about the reasoning behind that, it makes logical sense. If you're renting out a place, you price the rent at a big higher than the mortgage, so that your renter pays your mortgage, and you get a bit of pocket cash, which is a concept that is discussed in a forthcoming chapter.

So, traditionally, there's been an accessibility issue, however, this issue resides in the down payment portion of the funds required to purchase a home. Usually, it's a 20% down payment, which on a $300,000 home equals out to $60,000. I'd think there are very few people in their 20's that have that much cash lying around. So, to make homeownership more accessible, there are first-time homebuyer benefits put out by the Government that actually lower that down payment percentage to as low as 3.5%. These types of loans are backed by the Federal Housing Administration, and offer a much more accessible route to home ownership. It should be noted that with the good comes the bad, because you will be charged an additional mortgage insurance monthly, but within a year or two, you do have the ability to refinance so that you're able to get rid of that insurance payment.

Traveling. Now, one fact that is on the mind of most 20-somethings is traveling. I believe it's something about our genetics that makes wanderlust peak at this time in our lives. However, as is the case with all other goals, there's a clear distinction between wanting to travel, and actually making that a reality through sound financial planning. I think it's great for someone to say "2018 is going to be the year for me, I'm traveling EVERYWHERE", but I think that most people stop there, and then spend the rest of the year complaining about how they can't travel. This type of mentality is definitely something that haunted me for the first year I was out of school. I was spending so much money on Amazon desk cacti and succulents that, when my friends asked if I wanted to join them on amazing trips, I had to say I couldn't, simply because I didn't have any money. Cue FOMO. Basically, if you don't meticulously plan your financial life, and in particular the costs associated with the traveling that you're dying to do, you'll inevitably cut down on the amount of places you're able to see, just because you spending habits are out of whack.

It's no secret that traveling can usually be a very costly experience, especially since flights in and of themselves cost an arm and a leg. Apart from just taking you 2-4 weeks of PTO annually, there are innovative ways that millennials have found to travel. The first of a host of popular options, which is something many of my friends took to after graduating, is to seek employment abroad. There are entire industries in foreign countries based around English Language Instruction, and these programs usually only require a Bachelor's Degree from an American College or University. This avenue is particularly attractive because it provides you with a guaranteed income, places you in a foreign environment, and gives you accessibility to other nearby countries. Another point to make about this experience is that it helps build professional skills, and you get to meet likeminded individuals who also probably love to travel.

However, not everyone desires to have a job in English Language Instruction. By far, most people look to traveling as a way to explore outside of their regular 9-5. However, stateside, you'll also be able to find likeminded individuals to travel with, in the form of close friends, thereby drastically cutting the cost of trips by spreading it over multiple people. Traveling with friends is also an amazing option because it lets you continually strengthen the bonds of friendship, something that becomes increasingly difficult as you all start to build divergent lives. Some of the best experiences in my entire life have happened while traveling with friends!

Now, traveling internationally, or domestically, doesn't have to put a huge dent into your annual budget. A budget trip to a foreign country can easily be done under $1,000 if you fly out of season, and stay in an Airbnb (please leave hostels in your collegiate PAST), and spread out the cost amongst a moderate amount of people. Some helpful tips that I've gotten about finding budget flights is setting google status alerts for fare prices, in addition to utilizing websites like Hipmunk, that provide honest fare comparisons. I also religiously scrape my machine of cookies after each flight search, because I refuse to be up-charged simply because my browser knows that I'm trying to go to Bali in May.

Another thing that I found to be very true for myself as I've grown is that I'm more willing to pay for experiences, as opposed to stuff. When I was younger, and even in College, I used to purchase a lot of trinkets and mementos from where ever I was traveling. These costs ended up being $200 worth of stuff that got stored in my parent's garage. Now, when I travel, I just stay away from all of that stuff because I know that paying $40 for a ziplining tour will leave me with an amazing memory for the rest of my life, whereas a $40 tie dye t-shirt that says "Pura Vida" is going to be used as a dish rag by my mom in the near future.

Post-graduate education. One last topic that I did want to take a deep dive into is the concept of post-graduate education. It's a pretty common situation to work for a couple of years after you graduate, and realize that your true passion lies in something else, and something for which you'll have to return to school for. Many of friends from school worked as paralegals prior to going to Law School, as scribes before going to Medical/PA School, or in Industry prior to going to Business School. I think that in terms of finances, there's little you can do to "save" for graduate school, but there are intelligent ways for you to get other people to pay for your degree. Looking at the price tag of Medical School alone, it hovers in the hundred thousands, which is not a number that you realistically save in two years.

So, though it's difficult to save for graduate school, you can certainly play it smart and either have your employer sponsor your education, or conversely, looking into a state sponsored scholarship. I'm a huge proponent of avoiding school loans as much as is possible. In particular, I'm a bit aghast at the price tag of graduate education in this Country, so to tie yourself to a $150K loan is not a small decision, and it's one that will likely haunt you for the rest of your life. So, doing the appropriate research and figuring out how you can cut that down as much as possible is 100% worth the research. Some examples of getting other people to pay for your degree include Law firms sponsoring paralegals who go to school for their JD, the NHSC full scholarship for medical students who want to practice in high-needs primary care locations, and the myriad employer opportunities to get a sponsored scholarship for Business School.

In conclusion, these are just a couple of different examples of life decisions that you will face once you leave school and enter adulthood. Of course, like my buddy from school, your priorities might not align with any of these situations, and you might just want to pack up your camper and drive through the United States for five years. However, regardless of the goal, delineating the financial preparation that's necessary to accomplish those goals, making an actionable plan, and then committing to that plan is integral to your success.

<u>Key Takeaways</u>

✓ While investment is something that should be a priority, striking a balance between saving for retirement, and saving for big ticket financial goals is **<u>imperative</u>**.

✓ As is with any goal in life, with financial goals, an active imagine is not enough! It's a great advantage, sure, but without an actionable plan, your goals will never materialize because you won't have the financial foundation to stand them up! *Be intentional + specific* with financial planning in relation to your overarching goals.

✓ Thinking of buying a car or leasing? Where do you think you'll be in (5) years? Answer the latter and you'll be on the path towards figuring out the answer for the former.

✓ BUY a house as soon as possible. Really, how long do you expect to put your hard-earned dollars down for <u>someone else's</u> mortgage?!

✓ Hack the graduate school system IF you can. No, I'm not telling you to forge your transcript. I am encouraging you to find someone **ELSE** to pay for your education. #scholarships #companyfunding

Chapter 21:
Side Hustle Economy

You remember those "friends" in College that tried to sell you knives out of their trunks? No, not, like knives as a weapon, but the infomercial knives for cooking? Those ads where they got suckers to buy $500 worth of knives, and they had to sell them for commission? No? How about that empathetic friend who played you like a fool, and after you poured your entire life story out to her, she proceeded to try to sell you on a pyramid scheme leadership summit? C'mon, that's GOT to be familiar. Ok, how about this one, the "friend" that tried to sell you cheap leggings for $40, out of her basement? You know the ones that I'm talking about. If you don't have at least one acquaintance that tried to sell you on a pyramid scheme, I don't know what type of life you're living, my friend, but this type of situation was amazingly prevalent during my time in College, and in ways, even after College. I don't know what exactly leads people to buy into these obviously horrible ideas, but there's definitely tons of people out there that are devoting massive amounts of time to them. I'm convinced that, deep down, these people have to know that the whole thing is a sham, but at the same time, numerous people proceed to ruin personal friendships by attempting to "enroll" as many loved ones as possible! Perhaps worst of all, falling into doing "business" with these shady companies happens to seemingly normal people. My desire to discuss this phenomenon is based off of the fact that many of these people described these ventures to me as their "side hustle". I'm here to say that this, unequivocally, does not constitute as a legitimate side hustle.

Instead, I'm here to promote the TRUE side hustle, which is another type of investment that isn't usually viewed as a profitable, or realistic way of establishing a separate source of income, by most people. These side hustles, as they're lovingly referred to by the millennial generation, are ventures that are largely passion projects. Though people usually think of investment through the traditional scope of investing in stocks, bonds, and other securities, there's another, extremely important way of investment, which is, investing in yourself. And, one of the most creative, skills-building, and fulfilling way of investing in oneself, is by developing a side hustle! I'm a huge proponent of investing in oneself, and something that I've admired very much is friends of mine that have developed ventures, outside of their main job or career, and through that process, built so many creative skills. Your side hustle might be as creative as writing books or maintaining a blog about a topic that you LOVE, or it might be as out-of-the-box as finding lower priced items in department stores, and selling them for a profit online. The underpinning characteristic for me, that ties all of these ventures together, no matter how different, is the fact that it's driven from a place of authentic passion. Your values might drive you to express yourself through the written word, through music, or through finding a good deal. But, at the end of the day, what's most important is that the product that you're putting out is something that drives and motivates you, and so, in and of itself, results in a very authentic venture, which is the true mark of a side hustle. Forgive me, but I find it hard to see how anyone could be passionate about selling low quality leggings in a pyramid scheme type set-up!

Aside from providing an outlet for creativity and growth, which is so beneficial for your overall mental health and happiness, one of the great things about cultivating a side hustle is the opportunity to develop a separate source of income. We've spoken a bit about establishing multiple streams of income throughout this book, and described it in a variety of different ways. Some other ways we've discussed is house hacking, investing in rental properties, or creating a steady stream of monthly dividend payments. In today's age, one of the more popular ways to develop a separate source of income is through the development of a passion project, which can later be converted into a profitable venture. If and when your side hustle becomes profitable, you're opened up to a huge array of opportunities, which include leaving your day job for a passion project, or simply having additional cash each month with which to save and invest.

Qualitative Benefits of Establishing a Side Hustle. Personally speaking, I think that, outside of profit, the side hustle is a concept that's beneficial to a person in a host of different ways. Would it be surprising for you to know that most side hustles start during your lunch break? This is literally the amount of time you need, daily, to devote to something in order to see results. The secret to success here is consistency! Whether you developing an iOS app, writing a book, or creating a customized board game, these pursuits aren't that much of a time suck, and provide you with a consistent outlet for creativity. This last point has become increasingly important, as when asked about one of the prevailing reasons for unhappiness with one's work, people answer that their jobs don't provide them with an outlet for creativity. We move through our educational lives having countless opportunities to express our creativity through group projects, clubs, athletics, and more. But, large and in part, when you enter the professional world, there's seldom time to pursue creative desires because you're working a 9-5, doing tasks that often become routine. When that need for creativity isn't met in the traditional work space, simply taking out an hour a day to pursue a passion project adds so much richness to one's life!

Of course, the most important trickledown effect of consistency is that it allows one to build a skill, which could range from computer coding, to teaching guitar, to writing. It's interesting how most people don't realize how much they enjoy learning, until they're outside of school. When I was in school, I found studying to be a chore. I loved school, because of social factors, but I didn't really comprehend how much I enjoyed the act of learning, until I wasn't "forced" to do it anymore. Outside of the context of school, where I was suddenly "allowed" to learn about things that genuinely excited me, like writing, guitar playing, and finance, I found how much life the act of learning gave me, and how fulfilled I felt by adding a component of education into my daily life. Ultimately, developing these skills over time allows someone to build a product that they're immensely proud of, and reap from that experience the satisfaction that's provided through authentic accomplishment. Through the consistent devotion of an hour or two every day, you're building skills, a potential side income, self-satisfaction, creative experiences, and most importantly, a product that you're enamored with.

Examples of successful side hustles. While it might not be readily apparent, it's a fact that most successful companies didn't begin with the founders just straight up giving up their full-time jobs. Instead, the most successful companies in the world started as humble side hustles. I think that by now, most people are aware of the fact that Apple began in a garage. This company, which controls a massive amount of the world's wealth, started as a humble side hustle with the founders Steve Wozniak and Steve Jobs, who had a passion for creating a product that the world had never seen.

Similarly, in the age of technology, there are countless companies, like Facebook and Twitter that began as side hustles, when the founders already had full-time jobs. Perhaps a technology company that is more relatable to today's youth, as they've utilized it extensively throughout school, is Khan Academy. Sal Khan, the founder of this company, began it as a simple passion project because he had a desire to tutor his cousins who lived in a different state. Creating this online content to teach his cousins, while he was working as a full-time hedge fund analyst, later allowed him to develop the idea into a massive company that now reaches millions of users each year. One important thing to note about the success behind these major companies is, again, that driving theme of authenticity, paired with consistency. When you're authentic and true to your values, and create a product that's consistent with those themes, it'll inevitably be a product of quality, thereby increasing the overall chances of it becoming successful.

Sacrifices associated with side hustles. Now, developing a side hustle will require some serious sacrifices from a person, but in my view, these sacrifices are usually a way to enhance your quality of life, and so, they don't feel burdensome. When developing my skills early on, and giving my hand to the first side hustle I pursued, which was developing an iOS app, one of the biggest sacrifices I made was time. Back when I was in school, I was 100% part of the "Netflix binge" club. After a midterm, the biggest treat I had prepped for myself was finding a dope TV show, and binging it for two days straight. But, after I got a full-time job, I found that I only had a few hours to spare after work each day. There were certain things that I knew I definitely wanted to do, which was spend time with friends and family, play my guitar, and then, there was my side hustle. So, ultimately, I significantly reeled back my TV consumption. These days, I don't know what's going on in the latest season of Narcos, but to be honest, I'm probably much better off for it. When developing a side hustle, and maintaining a full time job, it becomes imperative that you start prioritizing what's important to you.

More so than time, one of the biggest issues I dealt with in respect to developing side hustles was my fear of failure. It takes a sizeable amount of courage to develop something, and then to put it out for all of your friends and family to see. Even still, putting it out there for complete strangers to critique is an even greater feat. There's a ton of second guessing that goes along with developing something that is 100% you. I often thought that all the work that I was putting in was useless, that the product I was building could never amount to the level of product that other professionals are creating, and that everything I was doing was for naught. Pushing through that, and not particularly caring about the overall outcome, but rather on maintaining a high level of personal authenticity in the product, helped me grow as a person by leaps and bounds. Even as I write this book, I doubt myself in that, will people find it useful and relatable? But, at the end of the day, I know that this an authentic work that's pointed at helping individuals who are in the same position that i was, three years ago, and so I'm proud of it. Pushing through that uncertainty, learning to accept that if you put in effort you will produce results, and remaining consistent are all hallmark mentalities that you develop by pushing through the process.

How to begin developing your side hustle. The first step of developing your side hustle is switching gears from being a "thinker" to becoming a "doer". One thing I noticed about myself during my first few years out of school was that I always had a vision of the person that I wanted to be, and the things I wanted to accomplish, but one thing that I never had was an actionable plan. I think it's awesome to have the idea to start a travel blog, or to write a cookbook, but if we're being real, that is always going to remain an untapped idea, unless you push yourself to action, and most importantly, remain consistent. So, really, the first step is to stop daydreaming as much, and to accept the reality that your goal of publishing a book, or performing live in a concert, or developing a subscription service is WHOLLY achievable. Once you develop this mentality, just start getting to work! Identification of your idea is a first step. Developing an idea might seem like a difficult task for some. This makes sense, as when we're in school, we are constantly encouraged to work within groups towards a greater good. Slowly, we get shuffled into careers, the overwhelming majority of which are traditional models where you work as a peg in a much larger organization. Because your thoughts are generally fixated on how efficient of a peg you can be, coming up with original thought can be a difficult task to approach. But, I believe that all of us have imaginative ideas within us that could easily be turned into profitable ventures. So, it's important at this initial stage to take the time to outline what you're passionate about, and come up with one or two ideas that you believe you could achieve, given the time.

The second step of creating a side hustle is setting aside time daily to work towards your goal. Encompassed within this daily work is a myriad different activities, based on your idea. You might set aside time to conduct user research, to write for an hour, or to compose music for an hour. However, it's important to remember that radical change in one's life is achieved by establishing consistent habits. The work of an hour a day, extrapolated over many months, can produce a wicked product! Most importantly, instead of always remaining fixated on the end product, learn to love the everyday process associated with your side hustle, as that's one driving factor that will always keep you motivated throughout the entire experience.

Ultimately, there are a massive amount of personal and financial benefits associated with the devotion of a serious amount of time to developing a passion project. Yes, there is the idea that, with time and iteration, this idea can become profitable, and it might even possibility establish a consistent stream of income for you, outside of your day job. There's even the chance that this stream of income could one day replace your primary stream of income, thereby providing you with a career in which you are your own boss. But, on a micro scale, side hustles bring about a ton of good in your life in respect to personal development. Through the devotion of an hour or two daily, you're able to express yourself creatively, develop skills, and create something that you are both completely responsible for, and immensely proud of.

Key Takeaways

- ✓ On often overlooked or underestimated type of investment is developing a **side-hustle**, or a personal passion that you lovingly build, which also has the possibility to start generating revenue.

- ✓ What does a side-hustle constitute? Really? Anything! You can write a book (*cough*), develop an app for running, or start playing gigs after learning guitar. The biggest factor is that it's something you're *PASSIONATE* about.

- ✓ Financial success really shouldn't be a central driver for the development of your side-hustle. Sure, it's something that can be seen as an added benefit at the onset. But, really, the main focus should be on the personal development that comes from having an outlet of creativity, growing a skill, and developing increased consistency within your life.

- ✓ How do I start? Honestly, the first step is to simply STOP daydreaming about it, and just **get at it**. Pen a chapter, sign up for guitar lessons, or write your first line of code. Come back to it daily, and you'll be amazed at what you create as time passes.

Chapter 22:
Psychology of Delayed Gratification

One of the prevailing characteristics that spells out success for someone as an investor is simply, patience. In particular, it's important to discuss the role that patience, and more specifically, delayed gratification, play within investment, because not truly embracing these ideals is what leads to the downfall of many young investors. Making this struggle even more difficult for today's generation is the concept of Social Media, and how it's literally rewiring our brains, and, subsequently, the way we think. I, like most people, was an early adopter of technology, because it plays such a prevalent role within the life of any modern young person these days. Along with adopting tech, I also definitely took, and take, part in the wave of different social media sites that market to young people including Snapchat, Facebook to a certain degree, Instagram, VSCO, and others.

If you're skeptical, I was there with you a couple of years ago. The first time I read something about the detrimental effects of social media addiction, in that it causes increased stress, anxiety, depression, and addiction amongst youth, I had a response similar to most people! I just thought people were blowing the issue way out of proportion, and that my occasional scrolling on Instagram wasn't an issue. Eventually, a friend of mine told me about an app that times your activity on various sites, and after a week, the analysis really made me step back. Apparently, I'd spent 14 hours that week on Instagram alone, not even including all the time I wasted on various other social media sites. This realization caused me to reflect on my experience and, as I've reflected on the effect that social media has had on me, on my friends, and on society at large, I do believe that it's caused us to shift mentally, and probably not in the best way.

We are a cultural species, and the large majority of us rely on the acceptance of others to validate ourselves, particularly when we are in our growing stages. Perhaps most alarmingly, the advent of social media has created a generation of people that have dopamine rushes based on what they're posting online. It's all too familiar to be sitting at your desk at 12 A.M. on a Tuesday night, when you know you have a midterm tomorrow morning, but you're too busy posting pictures on social media, and then addicting waiting for the associated likes and comments. Scarier still is the fact that all the while, these actions are causing actual chemical changes within our brain. Just like someone builds a dopamine pathway in their brain in association to more common addictions like cigarettes, alcohol, and other substances, so too are today's kids "abusing" social media.

This pattern, in turn, has created a new societal expectation of instant gratification. As soon as you post that new insta pic, you're waiting like some sort of lunatic to see if the number of likes you'll get will eclipse your last photo, I even have friends that will text me and ask why I haven't liked the photo that they posted 48 seconds ago. There's less and less of a premium put on building relationships via authenticity, and more and more emphasis put on this unreal depiction of one's life that they broadcast via social media. I speak candidly because I was definitely in that mindset during different parts of my life. So, no judgement really, and I use the term "lunatic", to describe myself as well, because thinking of myself doing that, definitely makes me think, "Wow, you were so *weird* then....".

Now, this culture of instant gratification has started to spill over to nearly every facet of society. In respect to how we socialize, we expect friends and family to respond to us immediately. As far as jobs are concerned, we're also acting in a haphazard, reward-driven way. You'd be surprised how many people subscribe to the attitude of switching jobs rapidly in order to see nominal changes in our pay, without really giving as much attention to the skills, relationships, or careers we're building. In addition, it's changing how companies respond to us as consumers. Netflix, which was largely a movie rental company up until a decade ago, became transformed by this culture of "Now! Now! Now!" and is now predominantly a streaming service. In this instance, I'd like to paint how the culture of immediacy can actually turn out some products that increase our productivity, and for that reason, might possibly have the potential for creating good. As is known, many people enjoy the subscription economy, and like that their groceries, movies, clothes, and all other necessities are delivered to them immediately, or in worst case, via two-day shipping. So, yes, in limited ways, immediacy can be good, because it can provide us with a higher level of efficiency within our lives, but I would stress that adopting this type of mindset in respect to investing can be catastrophic for one's long term financial health.

We also know that delayed gratification is linked with long term success in a variety of different ways. To really understand the concept of delayed gratification, one of the best ways it was ever described to me was through the example of the

Stanford Marshmallow Experiment. To provide you with a quick synopsis, the experiment was conducted on young children, younger than seven. These kids were put inside a room with a marshmallow placed in front of them, and they were given two choices. The first choice was to just eat the marshmallow now, and the other choice was to wait for fifteen minutes without eating said marshmallow, and if they made it, they'd be rewarded with another marshmallow. In the end, about a third of those kids resisted temptation, and got that second 'mallow. Perhaps the most interesting part of this experiment was what happened many years later. The head researcher, or whoever, followed these kids' academic trajectories and realized that the ones that had resisted temptation, and applied the ideals of patience and delayed gratification during that experiment, ended up being more competent, and scoring higher on their SATs than the other children, who had failed to be patient.

Now, I don't think that patience means intelligence. In fact, I'd go as far as to say that intelligence is always the runner-up to hard work, but that's a totally different topic in and of itself. However, I do believe that if you continually practice patience, and delayed gratification, you do end up with a better result, because you're continuously picturing the end state, and outlining the objectives you need to accomplish to get there. Perhaps the most destructive reason behind the instant gratification society, for me, is that it keeps people from developing the habits they need to accomplish long term goals, accomplishments that are closely linked with overall happiness. So, again, I don't think these kids ended up doing well on their SATs because of some link between patience and intelligence, rather, I think they did better because they were able to visualize a personal goal, whether that be having two marshmallows or doing well on their SATs, create an actionable plan to get there, and then have the resolve required for a successful follow-through.

Of course, building the resolve to follow through on any plan is an acquired skill for most, including me. Unfortunately I know a disproportionate amount of young people who don't utilize resolve to accomplish long-term goals for themselves, especially not long-term financial goals. One of the saddest pictures of how awry things can go if you bring this mindset into investing was shown to me during the whole Bitcoin hype. I knew of more than a handful of people that were, in my mind, extremely intelligent individuals, but then who would turn around and tell me that they thought they were going to be millionaires by year end based on their investments in crypto. However, as we all saw, cryptocurrency took a hit, and whether or not we can agree on if the bubble really burst, it's a fact that most investors who got in because of the hype surrounding crypto, lost out. Some of these intelligent friends of mine lost out on $20,000+! During that time, the best approach for someone, who I can only hope invested because they believed in the future of Cryptocurrency and Blockchain, would have been to sit still and hold, to have the resolve and patience to see a small investment blip through.

However, because many of these young crypto investors didn't have the skills built within themselves to establish resolve in relation to their investment, it led to a massive sell-off. As the stock market can show us, this mindset is definitely not a new thing, because fickleness might be the biggest characteristic amongst most investors. In fact, one of the biggest issues with prices in the stock market, is people selling off because they believe an impending drop is going to happen, and even though it might not have, it eventually does because people start selling off en masse.

Thankfully, in order to develop delayed gratification as one of the guiding lights in your financial life, there are a variety of ways to go about applying. First and foremost, you should have a clear vision of what you want in your life. As has been mentioned earlier in the book, the more specific your goal, the better. Don't go for "I want to live on the beach". Instead, approach it as, "I plan to live on a beach facing property in Los Altos that is a single-family home with three bedrooms, two-bath, modern decor, and a large backyard, by the time I am 35." Full disclaimer, I realize how corny that sounds, you could even go as far as to say that it sounds a bit narcissistic to have such lofty goals for yourself. In the end, it's just going to be you looking at these goals, so it doesn't matter what anyone else thinks about this, because this is a way of you telling yourself what you have to do right now in order to realize the dreams you have for yourself long term. Now, after making this overarching goal, you can then see how much money you need to save up in order to get there, and then divide that up to create annual, and even better, monthly milestones for yourself. Now, accomplishing monthly milestones will, of course, involve sacrifice. For the monthly goals I have for myself, I definitely make sacrifices that my coworkers don't. As great as it would be to eat out every day for lunch, or to be able to drive-in to work every day, instead of using public transportation, I make my own lunch, and I rideshare, because at the end of the day, I have a monthly savings goal to meet. Using a daily budgeting app is something that I've personally found to be very helpful in this area. By utilizing this app, I'm able to prioritize larger expenses in the month, and directly see the effect that those goals have on the amount of money I have to use on a daily basis. Finances, at the end of the day, are complicated, and we have 10+ transactions to deal with each and every day. Personally, I feel that, as much as you're able to automate this process on a daily basis, with periodic manual oversight throughout the month, the easier it'll be to stick to it, and in turn, the more habitual it will become. Overall, having the grit that's required to achieve these goals month-in, month-out will help transition you from a mindset of instant gratification, where you'd be selling stuff left and right, spending way too much money, and generally just making a total mess of your finances, to a mindset of fortification and steadiness, where you apply the education you have to a sound financial plan, that you believe in.

Overall, I believe that being able to subject oneself to delayed gratification, and forgo an instant win in place of a much greater eventual prize, is a mindset that is a great predictor of eventual health and wealth. Being able to hold your own, keep your feet grounded, and stick to a financial plan/portfolio that you believe in, through the inevitable ups and downs of the market, are hallmark keys to success within investment. Along with physical health, adopting delayed gratification techniques is also a great way to fortify your mind, provide yourself with the satisfaction gained by achieving personal goals, and, as a result, achieve a greater sense of happiness within yourself.

<u>Key Takeaways</u>

✓ With the rise of technology and the advent of social media, our society has slowly fallen more and more into the traps of expecting instant gratification, a trait that is detrimental to long-term goal projection.

✓ Having a sense of delayed gratification is strongly linked with success, as is explained by the Stanford Marshmallow Experiment, because it forces one to picture the end state, instead of just giving into whatever will make them feel good in the moment.

✓ How does this relate to investment? Panic selling. FOMO buying. Both of these concepts can be drawn back to a lack of personal resolve and an inability to see the benefits of delayed gratification.

✓ Lastly...is delayed gratification an innate ability? Do only "smart" people have it? NO! Hard Work >>> Patience, any day. Developing the ability to withstand conditions for delayed gratification, particularly within investment, is a skill that people should be continually trying to improve.

Chapter 23:
Establishing Keystone Habits

I think one of the most common habits that children are instilled with while growing up is brushing their teeth, or at least, one can hope... As children, many of these habits are either passively or actively impressed upon us. Some examples of passive habits, which sometimes tend to be a bit more negative, that become a part of us might be nail biting, as a result of seeing other adults or children in your life also bite their nails, or by the same logic, nose picking! Even the "good" habits impressed upon us by our parents don't really involve any active participation on the part of the child really, as it's something that's a forced learned behavior, and not entirely a desire.

Now, this trend definitely shifts as we start to grow into our adolescence and into young adulthood. People pick up good habits, some motivators behind which could be a passion for fitness or music. However, it's not always rosy, and as we grow, we also pick up bad habits, which can be subtle, like developing a proclivity towards procrastination, or they can be more extreme, like drug and alcohol addiction. As you move through life, you become a walking collection of this mix of good and bad habits, and some of the latter can truly become a significant hindrance in your path to achieving a level of personal happiness in your life.

Personally, I'm not a very introspective person, as by nature, I don't really have innate motivators within me to be reflective, rather, I prefer to follow whatever path I've set myself on. This tendency definitely proved to be a difficult reality for me when I was in College, and had branched itself into a host of bad habits that were really stopping me from realizing my true potential.

There's a variety of quotes out there that will explain how the contents of your day make up the reality of your life. At least in my case, there was definitely a ton of reading of quotes and pieces of advice that went along those lines, but I wasn't ever really internalizing the impact of that statement. However, whether I wanted to understand it or not, that tenant of reality was most certainly playing out in my own life. I didn't realize how much time within my own day I was letting go to waste, and as a result, how much of my life was going to waste. During school, I was a ball of bad habits. I didn't particularly have a passion for anything, aside from doing well on tests, which was really a passion for doing well so that other people would be happy with my performance. I, like many people, fell into the horrible cycle of waking up at 1 PM, going to bed at 6 AM, and it's crazy to say, but I think there were large swaths of time during my Undergraduate experience where I saw zero personal at all. I was basically just coasting, I wasn't looking at my daily life as an exercise as to how to improve upon myself, rather, I had the outlook that the day was a thing to "overcome", as emo as that sounds.

It wasn't really until after I graduated from College, that I started to become a bit despondent with my rate of personal growth, had a couple of moments of introspection, and listened to a podcast about habit formation that kind of changed my perspective on how I utilized every day of my life. Through this season of my life, I found that one of the best ways to overcome my own deep-seeded bad habits was to consistently work towards developing beneficial keystone habits. This podcast explained the concept of keystone habits, which are essentially "powerhouse" habits that lead a person to developing multiple other beneficial habits in their life. After implementing the basic advice in this podcast, which was to pick up one keystone habit, I saw more personal growth within myself in the span of 2-3 months than I'd seen in an entire three years, which was a crazy cool experience for me. I think for many people, there's an internal guide that leads them to always desire personal growth, but for the large majority of people, life can become sort of mundane, and consist of the same thing day-to-day. I think it's wholly possible for a person to ignore this amazing gift we've been given in the form of 24 hours a day to accomplish our most fantastical goals, and instead kind of just coast through life for entire decades, which is just a really a sad reality that you should earnestly work avoid.

So, personally speaking, the one keystone habit that I developed was simply daily journaling. I religiously kept, and keep, a daily journal where I outline my personal goals, or how I feel about a certain situation, or simply how great I thought the weather was that day. The concept of keeping a journal is one that I've known about my entire life, but one that I never had the desire to be consistent about. The reality is that if you keep a journal for a day, or for a week, it's not going to make much of a change in your life. The real appreciable change is seen as a result of relentless consistency. Keep a journal for 365 days in a row and you'll be left with a much better understanding of who you are as a person, what you want to accomplish out of life, and how to handle the million emotions you feel in a day, and as a result, become a more level-headed and competent individual.

Now, I'm not saying that journaling is the end-all be-all habit for someone to adopt in order to see a ton of change in their life. For me, the journaling led to a host of different habits that I now incorporate into my daily life. Journaling made me desire more reflective moments within my day, so I took up meditating, and I started to keep a mood log within my phone, both things that I do daily, and which help me understand myself in such a way as to enable me to be more consistently proactive and efficient with my life. After seeing how well I did at being consistent with journaling, I decided to take up guitar, which is something I'd always wanted to do, but never thought I had enough talent for. Three months in, I'm an all right guitarist, but still growing. In a few months' time, I radically changed from the person that I used to be, and none of this involved huge "A-ha!" moments like they do for others. Rather, I slowly changed my day-to-day living to incorporate more moments that allowed me to grow as a person. Part of accepting that these actions were now daily habits for me, helped me overcome my perfectionist attitude. I subscribed quite heavily to the "all-or-nothing" mindset, throughout most of my life. Whereas now, when I'm learning a new song, or I'm studying for an exam that I might not be doing that well at, I accept it, and I use it as a motivator to come back even harder tomorrow. I enjoy sharing with people how liberating it was for me to realize that all successful people fail forward, and that failure is something that you shouldn't run from. When preparing songs on my guitar, I routinely fail every single day for entire weeks before it comes to me. The first song I learned on guitar was Romanza, which is a Spanish love ballad.

When I first played it, there's a partial bar chord right in the middle of the song. My fingers are a bit small so, at first, that bar chord just never sounded right. In fact, it didn't sound right for an entire month. Struggling through that, keep a positive mindset, and finally getting past it helped me get over so many of the self-limiting beliefs I had for myself. My mindset before would've been just to throw my guitar away and not look at it for two weeks, and this is a feeling of frustration that probably resonates with most people. People don't share this mentality enough, because my focus on perfectionism, and my aversion to failure, led me to many years of self-doubt and zero personal growth.

Along with becoming more comfortable with failing towards success, I began to see more progress within myself, which made me think of myself as a much more competent person. The confidence that comes with the realization that you have unbounding ability sets your world on fire with the desire to go out there and just smash every goal that you ever envisioned for yourself. When I was so paralyzed by my inability to keep my perfectionist ideals, I was an insecure mess, and believed that I was unable to accomplish any goal, let alone the loftier ones out there that I really wanted to target. Prior to developing these beneficial habits in my life, and consistently struggling towards a goal, I always had this mindset that if I wasn't good at something right off the bat, that I was just incapable of doing that thing. These self-limiting beliefs had led me to a whole lot of inaction in my life. But, by consistently accomplishing goals over time, I'm now better able to say, "Well, why not me? Why can't I do that? Give it some time, and I can definitely do that."

I suppose that the most powerful, and the most important part of keystone habits, is that it's accessible to everyone and it is really, easy. Because you start out with one, singular habit, it eventually spills over into every facet of your life. The habit could be as simple as just making your bed every single morning, which is actually something that I am extremely passionate about, because it gives you such a sense of accomplishment, first thing in the morning. Caveat, I used to think that those people with 18 pillows on their bed were nuts, but I've started to see the method behind that madness! Common examples of keystone habits are exercising 30 minutes a day, giving up soda, adopting a visualization practice, or cooking your meals at home every day. Depending upon your needs at that time in your life, the keystone habit will differ, and again, based upon those needs, the direction in which you start to branch out your habits, will also be distinct from others.

Ok, fair, some of you might be thinking "This is a finance book, so why are we talking about journaling?" Though I'm still reflecting on it, I think my desire to develop keystone habits came from a place where I wanted to become an adult, and not feel as helpless as I did when I was in College and was a "child". So while it started out with journaling, one of the downriver effects of that journey was me becoming more competent with my personal finances. If personal finance is an area of deep concern for you, you might even want to start out with a keystone habit based in this topic. Particularly with investment and money management, because there are literally hundreds of different topics, and even more terms to understand, it can be an extremely daunting task to take upon oneself. I'm very much of the belief that if you try to take in information like a water hose and pummel yourself with it all at once, it can become extremely intimidating, and just like I threw my guitar away a thousand times when I became frustrated with it in high school, you might just throw away thoughts of money management, which can really exacerbate things.

Instead, start out with one manageable goal, and develop a keystone habit around it. Once of my first finance habits was paring my monthly expenditures down to about $750 a month. That left me with about $20 a day, and I used to keep, and still actually do keep, a budgeting app on my phone. Every time I made an expense, I'd enter it into the app, and I made sure never to go above an average of $20 a day, over the course of a week. At first, it might seem like I was wasting time because I was only doing this one thing, and I could be doing so much more like educating myself on investment, or starting to develop my portfolio. However, that daily habit, after a month or so, turned into another habit, where I'd read one finance article each day. And slowly, over the course of 5-6 months, I consistently kept a handful of habits related to personal finance that helped me achieve my overarching goals, whereas, if I'd tried to do all of this at once, I'm certain of the fact that I would've failed.

Now, I do want to take a moment to relay the importance of accountability. One of the biggest reasons I kept up with habit formation was through the use of a mobile app that tracks daily habit completions. Without that app, I wouldn't have been able to keep straight the 20 or so habits I juggle on any given month. As you apply those habits daily, some of them become a stoic fixture within your life, so you can stop trying to consciously remind yourself that you have to complete them. However, at least for the first few weeks, it'd be helpful to manage a habit log on a daily basis.

Overall, of course, I'd urge you, within the context of this book, to develop a keystone habit around personal finance. Ideally, it should be related to a specific goal, but should also be supported through daily implementation via the utilization of one to a handful of related habits. The real "life-changing" experience you're going to see as a result of accomplishing this goal, is through the daily action of executing your habits, and the down-river consistency you'll build over time.

<u>Key Takeaways</u>

✓ It's important to realize the significance of **introspection** and **reflection** in one's life. When we're young, other people largely make decisions for us, not providing us for much reason to reflect. But as we get older, we both have to assume responsibility for our actions, and grow more reflective of them.

✓ In order to start shifting away from habits that are limiting you, develop a **keystone habit**, which is a powerhouse habit that leads you to developing multiple other beneficial habits in your life.

✓ In relation to finances, one of my keystone habits was limiting my expenses to $20 a day, which, after I accomplished in a month or two, spilled over to the development of a budget that I religiously stick to , which spilled over to an increased interest in investment, so on and so forth. The key is sticking to <u>developing one new habit at a time</u>.

✓ A HUGE factor behind keystone habits is the acceptance of failure. Building a habit takes time, and failure is inevitable. ***But remember to fail forwards.*** Fail ten days in a row, but keep your resolve! The goal will materialize.

Chapter 24:
Habits of Wealthy People

Continuing our discussion on habits, within the context of this book, it's important to discuss the habits of wealthy people. When you start to look at habit formation to change yourself, you become more attune to the habits of the people closest to you in your life, as well as to the habits of society at large. Personally, this reflection has been very interesting for me, as I'm now able to observe how consumerism has created a paradoxical society in relation to how people portray their financial wellbeing. Let's unpack that thought, because my inner monologue is often a jumbled mess of words. What I'm trying to convey is that, in an attempt to seem "rich", people often dig themselves into financial holes, which is ironic. I was having dinner with three friends of mine the other night, and we were discussing consumerism and how it's both affected people in their life, and how it leads to the development of issues in a person's financial life, but also, more importantly, in their personal life as well.

Now, take university students in China. During dinner, my friend, who is from China, was telling me how loans are ruining the lives of a generation of Chinese women. And I started talking about how, yes, that's horrible, student loans are ruining the lives of millennials the world around. But then, she told me that no, education costs in China aren't unaffordable, and that the large majority of these women are taking out loans in order to buy designer HANDBAGS. How crazy is that? Please tell me you think that's crazy, because if not, no matter how many times you read this book, you're just never going to get it. Worse still was the fact that these women are taking out more predatory loans in order to pay back the initial loans, spiraling into loan hell and ruining their lives, for a handbag. What made them do that? As human beings are we naturally inclined to the beige beautifulness that is a Gucci bag? Of course not, let's be real those things are actually categorically ugly. What's doing this to these Chinese girls, and to mostly every member of society, is the rabid dog known as consumerism.

This is an extreme example, yes, but you definitely know someone who thinks like these girls do. Growing up, thankfully, my parents didn't put much of a premium on name brand items. We were a large family, of four children, that enjoyed shopping at Aldi, and utilizing hand-me-downs as much as humanly possible. I'm pretty sure that every single member of my family has worn certain items of clothing, all the way from my dad to my younger sister. Honestly, I'm very thankful for the fact that I was raised that way, because today, the idea of purchasing a handbag that has a certain symbol on it, when in all other qualities it's indistinguishable from one purchased at a much lower price, just doesn't register with me. However, I have friends who grew up in drastically different households, in which there *were* premiums put on brand name items. Households where you have $50,000 in credit card debt, but your mom isn't going to let you run around in Costco jeans, you're going to wear American Eagle. That child later becomes the young adult who, upon receiving a large student loan payment in their bank account, uses it to buy a brand new car, a purchase that loses value the second you drive it off the lot, but a loan that will potentially never lose value, and likely will keep getting more and more expensive to pay off. The root cause of the problem is two-prong. First of all, there is an unhealthy focus on how you appear to others. There's not a desire to be authentic, rather, there's a desire to show how you're superior to others. The second part of this issue is having little or no understanding of money, and thus training someone to be unappreciative, or not cognizant of the value of an earned dollar.

    In my personal opinion, you can't truly place 100% of the blame on these people, because they've been conditioned by their families, friends, and society at large to do irresponsible things like this. If you fall into this category, where you feel compelled to purchase things based on the image that they create for you, the best advice I could give you is that you just have to stop, and give up on this culture of "stuff". As paradoxical as it seems, there's such a liberation that comes from having less, because you're not trying to keep up with person XY or Z.

Instead, you make more authentic purchases that align with your values, needs and desires. Along those lines, I'm also very much of the mind that if someone intentionally saves for and purchases an $800 set of luggage, which is from a company that is known for providing quality products that stand the test of time, then that's a great purchase. There are name brand items out there that spell out quality, so shunning them altogether isn't what I'm advising. Instead, you should build a mantra of searching for authenticity, intentionality, and most importantly, balance amongst the consumer purchases you make.

With the multitude of horrible habits plaguing society and keeping them from developing wealth, it's a useful practice to analyze the good habits that will help someone climb out of the vicious financial cycle they're stuck in. Now, getting into the discussion of how a wealthy person behaves, first and foremost, we must decide, what's the definition of a "wealthy" person? Am I talking Warren Buffett wealthy? No, not at all. In my mind, a wealthy person is someone who is able to create a stable source of income, save wisely for retirement down the road, not be encumbered with the shackles of debt, and be able to make meaningful and intentional purchases with their capital. By that definition, you probably know at least a handful of wealthy people. I've relayed my sordid past with amazon purchases to you all. My breaking point in relation to these frivolous purchases came when I bought a $70 bonsai plant. Ridiculous! That plant died shortly after it was delivered, because again, I was making this purchase for all of the following, unauthentic and stupid reasons: 1) wow this bonsai will look awesome on my ig story 2) this will create for an awesome background for photos of my new EXECUTIVE desk 3) this looks cute, BUY. None of these reasons were based in my authentic desire to nurse a bonsai plant through to adulthood, or of my interests in horticulture, rather, I was looking at this purchase to create an image for others, as opposed to creating happiness for myself. After I made that purchase, I talked through it with two of my closest friends and through that guidance, I picked up on the first of many success habits that I developed in relation to making big purchases.

Essentially, if I see something that costs more than $20, and I have a desire to purchase it, I actually enter that expense into a budgeting app within my phone, that allows me to save money, per day, to make that eventual purchase. Now, days or weeks later, after I've saved enough money, based on the fact that I have a self-endowed allowance of about $20 a day, and whatever leftover cash I have day-by-day gets rolled up, I'll get a notification on my phone that I'm ready to make this purchase. 9 times out of 10, I have zero desire to buy that item anymore. Just taking that time in between the gut reaction of wanting to stuff it in your online cart and submit your payment, to the eventual reflection that this is something that you really don't need, is enough to save out on massive amounts of cash. Of course, there is that one off time when I see something that I just want, and in those cases, when I take the time to think about that purchase, my intentionality behind the process makes me value that item 10x more than I would've if I made that gut purchase on the spot. Of course, I'm not perfect, and I'll still make dumb purchases every now and again. But going from a place where I was using ALL of my discretionary income on amazon purchases, to a place where I slip up maybe once a month is definitive improvement. I owe all of this improvement to my continued practice of taking time to think about my purchases, which has become one of my strongest financial habits. Of course, I would urge you all that it's common sense that normal items do not fall under the purview of these rules. Don't wait a week to buy deodorant that could end up going badly for you...

Continuing this deep-dive into my personal habits, the second keystone habit that helped me overhaul my spending habits was making lunch at home. One of the things I enjoyed MOST about having a full-time job was my increased financial freedom. I went from a place where a Doritos locos taco was a real luxury, to being able to spend money on socializing, which of course, involved one too many brunches. As I've spoken about, it got to a point where I was eating out at lunch every. single. day! Again, it's difficult to appreciate the gravity of that decision when looked at as a single $12 lunch. But, extrapolate that over 20 work days, and you have $240 spent on food alone! On top of that, there were definitely weekend and weeknight dinners, and the amount of money I spent on social eating alone was around $400 a month, which is nuts! Personally, I don't drink alcohol, but if you do, this situation can become even more irresponsible, as buying a bunch of alcoholic drinks is usually a pretty expensive ways to spend an evening, and can burn a huge hole into your wallet.

And so, I made the intentional choice of preparing lunch at home for at least 2-3 days each week. The food sucked for the first, I'd say, two months. I didn't know how to cook, and I sad faced my way through my lunches as I slowly built my skills in the kitchen as well. Now, this ended up being a strong keystone habit for me, as I soon had an increased desire to use public transportation to cut commuting costs, and even started to rent audiobooks from my library in place of an audible subscription. Of course, all of these areas of saving are totally unrelated, but once I saw how much money I was saving on a daily basis by cutting my food costs, I had a desire to look at other areas of my life where I could trim some costs.

Now, there are definitely a ton of keystone habits out there to get you started and on your way towards developing a better outlook of your financial responsibilities. Of course, developing intentionality is a must. But, I think one of the strongest things one can do to figure out what keystone habits to adopt is starting by 1) reading and 2) surrounding yourself with likeminded people. Reading, whether it be through Money magazine or a heavy book on budgeting, is going to help you SO much. I was never a big reader myself. For some reason, for years, I built this personal image of myself in which I didn't enjoy reading, and preferred to watch TV and listen to music. I lived my life this way for 24 years prior to realizing how much I adored reading after finding books that helped me grow so much as an individual. Coming from a former nonreader who now reads 2 books per month, give reading a shot! The books I've read are better than any show I've ever watched, and yes, that includes "The Office". Making a consistent habit of reading about personal finance on a daily basis will go a long way towards helping you identify new habits that you want to incorporate into your life.

One par with reading, and increasing your education in relation to personal finance is developing a good network of supportive friends who you have goals in common with. When I was reading up and learning different concepts, I would ALWAYS bounce these ideas off of two of my closest friends. Get a group text going and text about all the crazy new finance stuff you're learning, because more often than not, your friends and family will help you see the negatives behind an idea that you might be prematurely gung-ho about! In the same way, they'll probably know of a couple different ideas that are related to something you're currently exploring. Essentially, multiple heads are much better than just your own.

Overall, developing sound financial habits is a journey that you will be on, forever. There's a steep learning curve at the beginning, but it's at this time that you'll see the most growth within yourself, as you'll be busy laying the foundation of how you make, spend, and utilize your money to create wealth. As you continue building upon that foundation, you'll become a savvier investor, and continue to increase your level of competency in relation to personal finance. So, again, to reiterate, Warren Buffett is not the ideal that most young people should aspire to live up to. Instead, look towards role models within your life that are able to hold down jobs they enjoy, afford housing that they're proud of, raise their families, partake in activities they're passionate about, and ultimately, build a retirement for themselves that allows them to leave the workforce at the right time. In my mind, that's the balanced success that defines whether or not a person "wealthy" in finances, and in life.

<u>Key Takeaways</u>

✓ **<u>What is a wealthy person?</u>** A wealthy person is someone who is able to create a stable source of income, save wisely for retirement down the road, not be encumbered with the shackles of debt, and be able to make meaningful and intentional purchases with their capital.

✓ Habits of wealthy people? Being mindful of their purchases, making intentional choices to curb costs (i.e. packing lunch as opposed to mindlessly purchasing), and overall, understanding the importance of being accountable + <u>in control of their finances.</u>

✓ One HUGE point - Don't fall into the trap of **consumerism**. Become mindful of your purchases. It's OK to make a one-time expensive purchase if it's based on personal happiness + quality. It's NOT ok to buy something so you can show it to others, the intentionality is skewed there.

✓ Develop a good network of supportive friends who have the shared goal of acquiring more financial acumen! **You are the average of your five closest friends.** So please, don't acquire 5 friends who max out credit cards to buy Wizards Tickets or buy the new Gucci bag.

Chapter 25:
The Concept of "Less"

When I was in College, my dorm room was pretty much like a war zone. Though my life was undoubtedly much less complicated back then, I somehow found zero time to pick up after myself. If you're thinking that this was perhaps born out of some rage-filled rebellion, where I was getting back at my parents for all the years they forced me to pick up after myself, you'd be wrong. In fact, my room was rather disgusting in high school as well, though my parents never really got after me too much for it. But, in College, that bad habit definitely got worse, and at times I couldn't even open the door to my room because there was SO much crap on the floor. I was a Resident Advisor, as well, and I'd make it a point to always have mediation meetings outside of my room, because honestly, it was a horrifying scene. I'm laughing to myself right now as I think back on one time where a student did actually catch a glimpse of my room, and the look of shocked horror is something I will never forget. Similar to my room, my life was pretty much a mess during those years as well, I was all over the place! Though I had little responsibility, and large amounts of free time in any given day, I always felt like I was losing it, and generally ran around in a frantic haze for those four years.

Eventually, I graduated College and started working as a K-12 Teacher, and on the very first day of school, II suddenly had a thought, "What kind of teacher am I, if I don't make my bed in the morning?" Completely illogical, made no sense, since when are these kids ever going to find out that my room looked like crap? Furthermore, why was I so concerned with the opinion of twelve-year-old's that I hadn't even met? Still, I had this realization that I was an adult now, and because I was an adult, I couldn't leave week-old food plates in my room any longer! Throughout that first six months of school, I made a concerted effort, each and every day, to keep my room clean. Slowly, I did go from being known as one of the most slovenly of my parent's children, to being one of the cleanest. I found that the more I kept my room, my closet, and my desk straight, the more clear my mind felt. It's also interesting, because at this time and point in my life, I rarely had any time to myself at all. I'd get up at 5 AM, teach until 3 PM, get home at 5 PM, and be grading and planning lessons right up until bed. Still, I found the twenty minutes a day to try to straighten my room, make sure everything looked pristine, and through that process, found a love for keeping things organized.

Now, I am aware that there is a ton of literature out there that explains the fact that "creative" people thrive on disorder. Sure, maybe some people like having stuff in every nook and cranny of their living space, and somehow "thrive" on that, but for 99.99% of people, I think it's the exact opposite. There's also a very famous saying "Clean space, clear mind", though I obviously never heard it for the first twenty-three years of my life. Still, gradually, I became a huge proponent of the fact that if you have a physical representation of disorder in your life, it leads to a mentality of chaos as well. I got so passionate about this subject that I even told my classes about it when I was teaching middle school. Of course, they all rolled their eyes as if I was their mom giving them another lecture, but, whenever I meet a young person who is having difficulty with their studies, I'm quick to ask what their room looks like, because I do believe that being unorganized is the foundation of being unprepared for all the challenges you'll face in life.

Now, I'm weird, so once I started getting into organization, I would read different blogs about cleaning, you know, what the best vacuum brand was, or if there were ways you could trick out your desk so that it allowed for hidden storage (stop laughing). One of these blogs put me onto the philosophy of Japanese Minimalism, which is more to less a way to generate a feeling of "more" in life more achieved through, simply, having less stuff. Though I'd highly recommend reading more about the intricacies and strategies associated with this subject, the essential idea is that if something is not actively utilized on a daily basis, it's not worth keeping. This idea really resonated with me, because even though I was spending time cleaning every single day, I felt like the "mess" continued to morph its way back into my life on a daily basis!

After reading about Japanese Minimalism, I adopted this practice into my own day-to-day living. At first, as is the case, the process began with a huge purge of items. There was so much crap in my room, and in my life, that I just didn't utilize, want, or need anymore. Of course, I'm not saying go all Armageddon on things and throw away mementos like childhood photos. The things that bring you happiness, even if you don't use them every day, should be retained, but at the same time, you cannot justify how 18 stuffed animals from your childhood bring you joy, because you're acting like a hoarder at that point. After this purging phase, and a reorganization of my closet, I didn't have to pick up nearly as much, and only really "straightened" up my room once daily, when I made my bed.

If you're someone that is looking to make this transition towards tidiness, I'd honestly urge you to start with the keystone habit of making your bed every morning, with stubborn consistency. You'll slowly move through the natural progression towards tidiness. Reading different opinions on how to go about the decluttering process, which are available on myriad different minimalism blogs, is also a wonderful practical guide towards discerning what items are important in your life, and what items would give you a clearer sense of mind, if you simply did away with them. The best part about this slow progression towards cleanliness, is that it extends beyond just your living space, and encourages you to be a cleaner individual at work, in your car, and just in life, in general. You raise your standards of what it means to have a clean and tidy workspace.

Perhaps the most important transition, in relation to personal finance, which happened as a result of me prioritizing tidiness, was a marked change in my outlook on consumerism. A friend of mine recently relayed to me how she'd had her mom purchase her these Coach sneakers when she in high school, and though they were a pretty expensive purchase that she'd begged her mom for at the time, she only ever wore those shoes once or twice, and then became unenamored with them. Just like those shoes, when I was decluttering my room, I came across countless items that I'd begged my parents for, or worked for myself, that I didn't have any joy towards. Three pairs of Air Jordan's from middle school that I'd saved up nearly $400 for meant nothing to me. A $100 North Face backpack, that I'd only purchased because I thought it would make me look cooler, that I'd used for the last two weeks of high school, and then never looked at again.

Countless Apple Bottom jeans and jackets that I'd worn obsessively for a two month span in 8th grade, and then stuffed in the armpit of my closet. It made me so angry at myself, looking at these items, and seeing the money that I wasted.

However, as difficult as it was to hold those bejeweled Apple Bottom Jeans in my hand and be angry with myself, I saw many other things while I was decluttering that brought me absolute joy, many of which were handwritten notes from friends, and pictures of the different places I'd traveled and experienced with my loved ones. Personally speaking, this is the point and time in which I realized that I'd much rather invest my money in creating experiences, rather than buying things. By investing more money and time into experiencing things, I was able to identify a hallmark truth of our lives, in that, we always remember how different situations shaped who we are today, but we seldom take a nostalgic view back at the purchase of an item. In addition, I use the word "invest" pointedly, because I think that when you utilize your capital to create new experiences for yourself, and broaden your mind, this is an investment in your personal capital, something that we will explore in further detail in the forthcoming chapter.

Around this time in my life, I also decided to seriously cut back my spending on bogus "goods" like the bonsai trees and succulents mentioned throughout this book, and instead, utilize my money to save for both traveling, as well as experiencing places and activities that I hadn't before. It just makes so much more sense to me that a trip I take with friends will be a memory that will stay with me forever, whereas $500 worth of clothing is something that I will likely regret, or forget. Don't get me wrong, I'm not a hippie that lives in the woods and holds anti-consumerism signs outside Wall Street. Nor am I anything close to a minimalist that only owns three spoons. I believe in the consumer economy, and I am an active participant who still buy a variety of goods every month. But, I'm no longer frivolous, rather I'm much more selective of the goods that I buy, and I make sure that every purchase that I make leaves me with a resounding feeling of satisfaction, as opposed to remorse.

Overall, I do believe that living with less fills someone life with so much "more". It's liberating not to be tied to online shopping, and to be able to have the self-control to only make one or two clothing purchases a month. It's freeing to be able to spend $750 on a budget vacation, have enjoyed every single second of it, and be left with memories for a lifetime. And most importantly, it's empowering to know that regardless of what's going on in the social media stratosphere, you're satisfied with the simplistic way with which you live your life.

<u>Key Takeaways</u>

✓ "Clean space, clear mind." That saying is **#REAL**. Organizing your life starts by organizing your physical space.

✓ Part of my journey towards tidiness led to a marked financial change in my mind, as I started to take steps away from consumerism. Brands and companies make it so that we become hoarders. Instead, a much better approach is to look at high quality items, regardless of brand, that you <u>NEED</u> and that will help you take one step away from #HoarderLife.

✓ When looked at holistically, **experiences >>>> things**. Choose to spend your dollars on creating memories, as opposed to creating clutter.

✓ Living with less is **<u>LIBERATING</u>**. Breaking the dependency on online shopping, with all of it's dopamine filled highs and lows, is in and of itself a HUGE victory for the modern shopper.

Chapter 26:
Developing Personal Capital

One of the biggest issues I faced after starting my career was finding the motivation to pursue things outside of the scope of work. Really though, I feel like that has been a prevailing issue all of my life, and in general, is a pretty common problem for most people. If you think about it, most of us have an ingrained desire to please others. If I think back to my time in school, I didn't do well in my classes because of any innate desire to learn about Newton's however many laws of physics, rather, I wanted to show my teacher I could be a good student. This makes me sound like a dork, I understand this, but that was honestly the reason I tried so hard in school, because I wanted to make my teachers proud of me.

This proclivity towards "people pleasing" is something I dragged along with me into the workplace. If my boss ever had a deadline for me, even if it was only two hours out, I would move heaven and earth in order to meet that deadline, and I made sure to prioritize it over every other thing in my life to the point where I'd put my phone on airplane mode! I mean, I still do that, because I think there are certain people pleasing characteristics, like this one, that are partly advantageous in the workplace. Similarly, I had a desire to maintain a high level of harmony in the workplace, as I did when I was in school, which is also a by-product of having a largely submissive nature. And though I don't want to get into an in-depth discussion about the psychology of people pleasing, I will point out that, mostly, this is not an advantageous mindset to cultivate. People pleasing brought me into this place where I would profusely apologize to others, be overly thankful, and be extremely averse to confrontation, to the point where I'd let things fester well beyond reasonable time limits. Of course, after identifying that these things were really hindering me, I pushed myself to be more authentic in the workplace, thereby not being as embarrassingly apologetic as I had been, in addition to actively seeking out areas where I could improve upon my mediation skills in relation to confrontation. All of this continues to be a work in progress for me, as it is for most young professionals, and in that spirit, I would urge you to remember, that if you're terrified in a certain situation, most other people are, too. Take some comfort and confidence in that!

Now, going back to the point of this discussion, I've always had "interests" outside of work. But, I say interests, because they always just remained something I was interested in, but never translated into something that I took action on. In school, I always had a fantasy of being a great guitarist, and when I started my career, I continually thought of becoming more involved in volunteering organizations. Of course, through the first 22 years of my life, I never found the time to study guitar. And, likewise, throughout the first three years of my career, I didn't volunteer once. Instead, I continued to have this very laser focus on schoolwork, and as time progressed, on my tasks at work. Putting 100% of who I was into work, while being a natural tendency, left me with an extremely high level of stress and anxiety, and even though I often felt burnt out, I kept pushing, much to my detriment.

When I turned 24, I kind of had a moment of reflection in that, I'd met so many deadlines in my life, gotten the right "numbers" in school, prepared so many reports and tools at work, and I had absolutely nothing left for myself. I'd spent precious years of my life completing tasks for other people, and I'd neglected to accomplish much for the one person who should matter the most, me! I'm not trying to get overly emotional here, but neglecting yourself is something that everyone does. When you derive personal joy and a sense of accomplishment from helping others, this tendency tends to become even more pronounced.

One of the biggest factors that led me to this personal discovery and gradual transition towards caring more for myself, was comparison! I'm the first proponent of the fact that everyone has their own timeline, and that YOUR timeline is the only one that matters. And so, for the most part, I don't think that comparing yourself to others is a practice that's normally very productive. In fact, I think it's an extremely regressive behavior to obsessively "watch" the lives of others, become despondent within yourself, and thereby halt your progression even more. But, in the same sense, I believe that, to a point, comparison does play a strong role in positive motivation. But, I think the nexus between positive vs. negative effects derived from personal comparison lie with the source of comparison. Of course, if you're comparing yourself to a 22-year-old Instagram Mogul, you're probably going to feel pretty crappy about the trajectory of your life. I don't give in to that fad, and training yourself to detach from social media in order to escape from that is a good practice. Instead, I do take personal inspiration from close friends and family who act as role models to me. And so, at this time in my life, I had a close friend that was cultivating a plethora of beneficial skills in his life, and I was astounded at the personal growth he'd seen as a result of both cultivating these skills, and of course, building them consistently over a long period of time.

So, I gave in, and even though I had doubts about how a guitar class could do anything to change my life when I felt so crap about it, I still went. And, truly, building that one skill radically changed the way I felt about myself. Before, even though I'd spent so much time developing tools for my clients, as soon as those projects were over, thanks were exchanged, and a compliment or two was thrown my way, I crashed. There was nothing left to show for all of that work that I'd done, for all of that part of me that I'd given to that project. More than a handful of times, I felt that an entire two to three months of my life had been for naught. Me feeling that way was largely a result of having poor balance. Because I poured my everything into my work, I felt despondent when the results, which were positively balanced results, didn't match my very unbalanced amount of dedication. After developing hobbies outside of work, however, like learning guitar, tutoring students in programming, and taking the time to throw myself into new experiences with friends, I found that developing my personal skills allowed me to feel so much more satisfied with life in general. And, yes, even though I was taking time out for me, I was still able to operate at the same level at work, but now had so much more richness and satisfaction with my own life.

Looking at the process, when looking to invest in yourself, there's a billion ways to go about it, each of which are personalized to a specific person's desires. You can start by simply taking the time to read, or meditate, or learn a new sport. You can have lofty goals like writing a book, or creating a videogame. The most important components of developing skills are 1) a level of immediacy and 2) consistency. I think the first rule is one that people struggle with, because they can't bear to prioritize themselves over the hundred things that other people require of them, but it's of utmost importance that you carve out time DAILY to develop yourself.

Imagine a life lived where you use all of your time to create budget reports for a large company. Sure, you develop relationships with your coworkers. But, the ultimate impact of that work is null in respect to who you are as a person. People move on, and once you're done with this job, no one will remember you. But, if you learn how to play a couple of sick riffs on a guitar, and amaze yourself with what you can do in relation to a hobby that you love, this is an accomplishment that's going to be impactful for you, forever. Likewise, it's so hard for me to see people choose careers over developing personal relationships, because I feel that regardless of how amazing your career becomes, there's always going to be an emptiness that it cannot fill in respect to quality, personal relationships.

In addition, try to avoid looking at developing yourself as a tradeoff between skills building and your quality of work. Taking that time out daily to develop yourself is going to increase your level of happiness and self-satisfaction, thereby allowing you to create even more impact in other parts of your life, like work. In my experience, developing hobbies has helped me mellow out quite a bit from the neurotic person I was in College. In fact, it's helped me better control my levels of stress and anxiety, and overall, create a much higher level of authenticity with every person that is a part of my life.

    At the end of the day, I think the most important investment principle you should take away from this book is that investing in yourself is the only surefire way to happiness. If you're anything like me, and enjoy utilizing both your skills of empathy and compassion, it's so important for you to realize that, until you show yourself an authentic level of compassion, you're never going to be able to practice that with others. I, like most people, still struggle with this balance. I still struggle with not wanting to pursue creative endeavors, like writing or practicing guitar, when I have stressful days at work. But, loving yourself enough to cut yourself some slack when you're trying so hard and things aren't working enough is important. Cultivating a mindset of happiness and of worthiness is also a predominant factor in relation to finding the consistency to pursue beloved qualities. Overall, investing in yourself is the most impactful way for you to see an increase in your quality of life. Just as you carve out time for others, begin prioritizing time for you to build skills and enjoy hobbies that provide you with a greater degree of happiness in your life.

<u>Key Takeaways</u>

✓ Pursue your personal goals **as passionately** as you pursue tasks for others. Just as much effort as you put into building a new budgeting tool at work should go into mastering the new scale you're learning on guitar. Personal passions do NOT take a back seat to professional obligations.

✓ Developing yourself should be AS **immediate** a need as doing task A, B, or C in relation to your year-end promotion. If you don't prioritize personal development, entire years of your life can be wasted in complacency.

✓ Don't look at personal development as a *trade-off* in respect to producing quality work products. Learn to bucket parts of your day for work activities, and to keep parts of the day just for yourself. They aren't mutually exclusive, having one doesn't mean you can't have the other.

In Closing

Thank you for joining me on this journey on learning the basics of personal finance! A couple of years ago, managing and growing money is something that I scarcely knew anything about. In writing this book, my main prerogative was thus to provide a concise, and centralized location for a basic education in personal finance, pointed at someone who is currently in the shoes that I was in a couple of years back. I'm empathetic to the young professionals who come from non-finance backgrounds and who don't have a functional knowledge of personal finance. People who, when asked, wouldn't be able to expand upon the distinctions between a 401(k) and a Roth IRA. So, it is my greatest hope that I was able to reach a couple of those people within this reading audience, and enable them to confidently lead discussions on finance, but more importantly, confidently take up the reigns of their own financial responsibilities. If you'd like to continue to learn more about personal finance, and peruse daily articles please visit my blog http://millennialfinance.com!

Made in the USA
Middletown, DE
15 June 2018